LOVE IS IN THE HAIR

LOVE IS IN THE HAIR

A Journey of Setbacks, Scissors, and Self-Worth:
How I built a Life in Beauty from the Inside Out

ANNIE FISHER

Published and distributed by Soul Speak Press
An imprint of Merack Publishing

ISBN: 978-1-958472-32-3 (eBook)
ISBN: 978-1-958472-31-6 (Paperback)
ISBN: 978-1-958472-33-0 (Hardcover)

Cover Credits
Photography:
James Cheng, Shelly Borga, Carlos Cruz
Hair:
Annie Fisher
Models:
Michaela, Anjelika, Adrianna, Erika, Haley, Mariah, Haily, Sara
Makeup artists:
Ryann Brady, Rick Toth, Kendall Faith Jacobsen, Cassie Bledsoe

This work is nonfiction and, as such, reflects the author's memory of her experiences.

To all my creatives out there who have ever been told that being a hairstylist isn't a real profession and who are finding the courage to follow their dream anyway—I see you.

May this book be a guide and inspiration on your journey.

Annie

CONTENTS

ACKNOWLEDGMENTS

I HAVE NOT GOTTEN TO WHERE I AM TODAY ALONE. There have been many people at each stage of my journey that have cheered me on and supported me in ways I could have never imagined.

I'd like to say thank you to my teachers from Marana High School who didn't ask for details, only offered a safe place to cry or even hide at times. They provided resources and encouragement while I went through some of the unspoken challenges at the darkest days of my life, and they have continued to be a light in my life. Thank you Peggy Korte, former director of the Teenage Parent Program; Linda Zello, former English and journalism teacher; Peggy Figueroa, former director of the Teenage Parent Program nursery. You were all a life saver in more ways than you will ever know.

Thank you to every employee who has been part of AFH Salon. From the front desk to assistants to stylists—thank you for taking a chance on me and the vision I held for us. You helped me grow not only as a leader but as a person. However our time together ended or however long our time together was, I hold gratitude for it. And to my current team: Your trust, creativity, and investment in our culture inspires me to keep going.

Thank you as well to every client who has ever taken a seat in my chair. Whether you came once or have been with me for years, your trust and belief in my work have meant everything. This group includes my friends who were my hair models early on and who are now my hype squad and biggest fans. My journey as an artist is woven from each of those moments, and I'm endlessly grateful.

Roy, my husband and partner in all things, thank you. You embraced not only who I am as a person, but also that my work is woven into me. You encouraged me at every leap, at every risk, and at every moment of self-doubt. Your support and faith in me fills a void. I love you . . .

INTRODUCTION

I INVITE YOU TO JOIN ME on a journey where the art of the hustle meets self-love, learned through lessons in entrepreneurship, which took me from just surviving to boldly thriving.

This book is also an additional way to heal myself, as well as a way to express gratitude to those who have supported me along my personal and professional journey. But mostly, I want to encourage other imperfect people, like me, to keep going and remind them to allow their inner voice to be one of the loudest voices they listen to: Trust it. What I know, at my core, is that we are all connected; relationships are how every single one of us gets to be who we are. I hope through this book you can reflect on each of your interactions, no matter how brief, with a deeper understanding of how they can leave a lasting influence. These experiences shared with others can either be lessons or blessings, but either way, they will shape how we move in the world. I hope what I share in these pages allows you to feel connected to me through my story, because maybe you see yourself too, and just maybe it will lead to us connecting IRL. I write because I have seen how fragile life is, and the side effect to this is the need to live with urgency, this opportunity is a privilege. I have lost so many people unexpectedly, to begin with my father at eight years old and because of that I know I want my story to be told by me today, because tomorrow isn't promised.

This book is a love letter to all versions of myself. I'm so proud of the woman I am still becoming, nearly fifty years old with no sign of completion yet. This former teen mom refused to be counted out and fought like hell to break out of the box the world had for me, which included generational trauma and patterns. I write this book as a love letter to my partner for seeing me and holding space so I can heal and shine, and as a love letter to my children who grew up *with* me, to remind them that I am grateful for their grace. I know they did not always get the best version of me as an unhealed teen mom. And finally, I write this as a love letter to this industry that has been more than I could have ever imagined, personally and professionally.

In a nod to my industry, I want to mention that this book isn't full of original ideas, but of themes that are consistent across salons, cities, states, and even countries. Because our experiences behind the chair share fundamental similarities, I wanted to give my industry friends, mentors, and people who genuinely love our industry a chance to share their own experiences and love letters. This comes from a place of community for me: I am grateful for this platform and couldn't imagine not bringing some friends, or at least their voices, along. So sprinkled within these pages, you'll find a wide range of industry and client experiences, and I hope this serves to further bolster your own journey, love, and passion in hair.

I am grateful for the chance to take you on my journey, which hopefully leaves you inspired in case you are asking yourself, what is my next big thing? Or perhaps it might just help you lean into contentment and gratitude for being exactly where you are.

I want to leave you with the quote I used in my first submission for a hair competition, and it rings just as true today. It inspires me and offers me accountability to my craft . . . I hope it does for you as well.

With love and light on your journey,

Annie

"I promise that my personal tragedy will not interfere
with my ability to do good hair."

—ANNELLE, STEEL MAGNOLIAS

CHAPTER 1

MY ROUTE TO HAIR

Long Hair: *Long hair* generally refers to strands of hair that extend past the shoulders, though the specific length considered long can vary based on cultural norms and individual preferences.

Across cultures and throughout history, long hair has held diverse meanings, often symbolizing strength, power, virility, status, and even rebellion, with interpretations varying significantly between societies and genders.

LET'S GET IT STARTED

I, like many girls of the '80s, grew up playing with my beloved Barbies. Their long silky (often blonde, unlike mine) hair was the part I liked playing with most. While other girls were busy picking out hot pink rubber heels the size of my pinky nail to coordinate with Barbie's latest evening gown, I was visualizing what I was going to do to her hair. The styling products I would sneak from under the bathroom sink didn't perform the same in Barbie's synthetic strands as it did in my hair. I was always so frustrated to experience the lack of shape that left her hair white and flakey. The fact that I couldn't figure out how to fix her hair is something that still stays with me. I am a fixer and still struggle accepting that some things just have to stay broken or unfixable. In an act of desperation, I would bring Barbie with me to the shower and in tandem to my own hair washing, I would scrub suds of VO5 into her little plastic scalp and then lovingly dry her head with a washcloth when our shower was complete. Unfortunately, her hair never looked the same as it had prior to my treatments. I didn't know it then, but Barbie's hair was my introduction to creativity, art, and how I could use my hands to express my voice through hair.

I would try to transform the long hair using whatever I could and would learn the hard way that her hair melts when using a curling iron. My ideas for an elegant updo or adding curls never quite translated to Barbie's hair; instead she often looked like she had a matted mess on her head. If you saw the Barbie movie that premiered in 2023, Weird Barbie and her many versions were the ones that lived at my house! These experiments led to a lesson in natural consequences: Once Barbie got her bob haircut to remove the mess I had made, it would not grow back. The way her hair was sewn into her head didn't allow for a cute pixie cut either, so my last resort was to shave her head. Ultimately, I was left negotiating for another Barbie so I could start the process again. The request for more dolls wasn't always successful unless it fell around my birthday or a holiday. Although when my sister came to visit she would bring hers for us to play with, and that was fun, and not just because of the Barbie.

I grew up in a blended family, which allowed me the opportunity to experience being a big sister. I always refer to my sister as non-bio, because there was nothing about us that was "step." She was and is my family. I am two years her elder, and we spent holidays and summer breaks together; I loved it. She was the total opposite of me. She was being raised in Southern California with her mom. She took dance lessons and was a cheerleader—all things feminine and girly, she was so beautiful to me, as she still is. I, on the other hand, was a total tomboy being raised in Tucson, Arizona. My interests were sport related and centered around animals and the outdoors. Our love for Barbies was the one thing we had in common.

Growing up in the desert heat, hair and clothing to me were about function and ease until I hit those tween years. I loved long board shorts and T-shirts, all the better to play whatever pickup game was happening at the park. I look back at photos and laugh that the hairstylist my mom and I would go to must have been offering to buy one adult haircut and get a child's cut for free. Or maybe I was just at the age where I wanted what my mom had. Different versions of bobs, pixies, and, yes, a mullet happened too; it was the '80s after all.

I was about ten years old when my mom repartnered. He had strong opinions pretty quickly about how we looked as a family, from me having to grow out my hair, to how we dressed, and even how we ate. I was of the generation that, when my hair was long enough, I slept in rollers the night before school or family photos; I hated it. I would also protest having to wear a dress for these occasions. Middle school was a bit of a turning point where I started to embrace products and express myself through my hair in a more traditionally feminine way, from scrunching my waves for what I called the "Top Ramen" look to hard-gelled curls to the overly teased Aqua-Net sprayed bangs that wouldn't have moved in a windstorm. Sporting such a high volume of products in my hair meant that I, along with my friends, was highly flammable. It was a vibe.

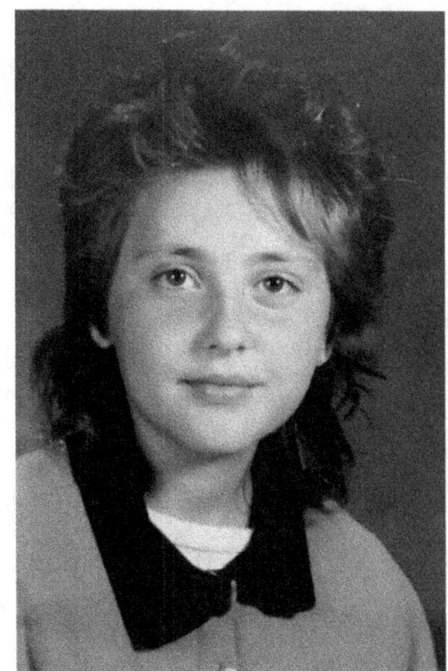

I remember eighth grade graduation being the first time that I picked a skirt for a special occasion, it wasn't forced on me, and I was excited to lean into being a "pretty" version of myself. It was in that moment that things shifted for me, just a little bit; I loved the oversized T-shirt and baggy-jeans sporty look during the day at school in contrast to my highly-styled hair, and I loved the shock and awe of showing up at eighth grade graduation wearing something more fitted and embracing my curves. This duality followed me through high school, highly-styled hair with little to no makeup, and I tended to lean into oversized clothing. Then when the opportunity would present itself like a school dance, I would go high glam, wearing elaborate gowns and blinging accessories, completed with an updo hairstyle and glam makeup. It always felt kind of like a Cinderella moment; I was unrecognizable from Annie during the day, in common clothes. I loved the drama and shock of my peers and teachers when I walked into the room, transformed. The power of clothing, hair, and makeup.

Being a big (non-bio) sister allowed me another muse. She was a good sport, but I knew with the strict home we grew up in, the girls-have-long-hair rule limited my creativity. My sister had beautiful long dark hair, on the straighter side. She would let me brush, curl, and pin her hair up whenever I wanted to. While my sister's hair was my creative playground, it was listening to her talk about her latest dance competition and latest happenings that most prepared me for my role now as a hairstylist.

Barbie remained my getaway into glam as a kiddo. Other than Barbie I didn't play with dolls beyond my toddler years.

Barbie allowed me to play being grown up, act out relationships from my perspective, and role play being a woman who could speak up for herself, which was different from my experience growing up; mostly I was in a house that followed the don't-speak-unless-spoken-to rule. These outlets and my connection to the animals on our ranch taught me the much-needed skill of building trust through touch with another being. Because my sister only visited a couple times a year, the horses and dogs on our ranch became my constant companions.

We had mostly Paint Horses, the ones that looked like they had walked straight out of a western movie, and they required a lot of regular grooming and maintenance because we bred them to sell, and also showed them. This was a different outlet for me, built on touch, trust, and unspoken connection. Because animals are so in tune to our energy, I had to learn about consent. This was my first lesson in how energy transfers. I could feel when they were off and needed a slow approach; sometimes I could dive right into touching, petting, brushing, and grooming, other times we had to have a slow warm-up that could look to an outsider like a standoff. On days like that, I knew I probably wouldn't be able to get the horses to consent to my favorite part—playing with their hair. Their manes and tails could be cut, braided, twisted in knots—I loved it!

While I flourished in my childhood with animals and their hair, there were parts of a traditional learning style that were hard. I really enjoyed being active and using my hands so school felt boring at times. Sitting in class to work on math problems did not provide the instant gratification I craved from doing something creative.

That being said, these kid-to-adolescent years deserve an acknowledgement without a play by play: Working with the horses or being at school offered me respite from my house where it was like walking on eggshells, and I witnessed and survived various abusive behaviors. There was addiction taking place in our home. I had my animals as my chores, as a hobby, and ultimately, as a safe place to escape. I worked hard at keeping up my grades to avoid any additional trouble and stay off the radar. These years showed me how strong I was because I had to survive each day. The challenges I faced at home taught me to lean into having faith and hope that one day I could make a life for myself outside of this dysfunction. I kept believing in the impending freedom to make choices for myself. I learned to listen to my gut and trust it when things felt off or just plain evil. Because of the stress over this time, I ended up dealing with health issues in my adult life, a diagnosis later of PTSD was one, and a strong need to have peace. I had a lot to unlearn and intentionally sought out examples of womanhood, motherhood, healthy relationships, and success that I hoped for myself. I am resilient and learned how to become resourceful, too, as a result of those years.

Fast forward: I'm seventeen and a teen mom. I left home after my stepfather passed unexpectedly, and suddenly, my first thought—we were all free! My mom was free, too, and wanted to figure out her next steps on her own. She suggested that my son and I stay with my boyfriend's family. I was still in high school but was left on my own to figure out how to provide for us. At that time I didn't have another option, and while the idea sounded horrible to me, I had no other choice. I hated needing this help, and I wasn't comfortable in their home. While I was grateful they took us in, I knew I wanted to get out on my own as soon as I could. So I started job hunting. The local mall had all the cool stores, and as I strolled down the walkway, pushing my son in his stroller, making a mental pros and cons list of applying at each store, I realized I was being drawn to Glamour Shots. They were hiring, and their ad claimed no experience was needed for an entry-level position. I considered other stores my friends were working at, but knew I had to give this a try first. Glamour Shots offered makeup applications, hairstyling, and a photography session wearing, what was considered then, a high fashion outfit. I had these photos done once with my mom, and they had made me feel

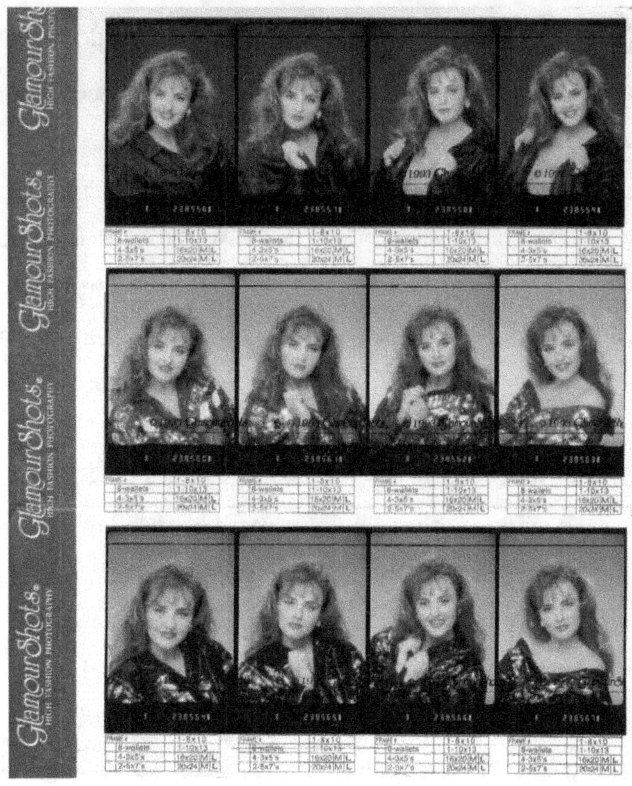

so beautiful. I really liked how I looked during the photoshoot, and I was excited for a chance to do that for others. I had an inexplicable level of confidence that I would be great for this job, and that is what I told them when I applied.

Against all odds, I got the job. It was the beginning of my understanding that life is filled with contradictions. Although I was a tomboy through and through, I had this fascination, borderline obsession, with working in a fancy place where I could help people look and feel their best. It was here where I evolved, both inside and out, settling into what would become one of my life's greatest mantras: *Beauty is available to EVERYONE, because it is inside us.*

I was so nervous and really wanted to do a good job, so much depended on it: I needed to pay my rent, gas, and learn how to cover our basic needs. My son was able to attend the nursery at my high school where I was a part of the teenage-parent program—TAPP. Thank goodness for Marana High School (MHS), TAPP, and the childcare it provided. My boyfriend and I found a small, cheap place close to school to get us out of his parents' house after a couple months. He was a year older than me, having graduated from MHS the year before, and was attending the local community college and working part-time. So it was out of necessity, but also this indescribable place of excitement, that I spent my first few weeks shadowing another employee at Glamour Shots. I entered the mirror-laden, hairspray-filled space and learned how to present the photos, assist the photographer during the shoot, and help people select their wardrobes before their picture was taken. The wardrobe consisted of wraps that offered some sparkle or sheen and leather jackets and feather boas in a variety of colors. I learned how to schedule sessions, cleaned a lot, and the most exciting part: I received hair and makeup training. In reflection on this time, it started my journey of healing, self-acceptance, and was really the first time I entered into the world as a creative person.

I was able to draw from playing stylist with my sister and building trust through touch with my animals, to learn that wanting to feel or look beautiful was something to be embraced, not embarrassed about. I practiced what I was taught, and not surprisingly, I was good at it. The confidence I received as I helped others define their beauty and play dress-up was a surprise to me. I watched them feel good about themselves, and in return, I felt good for them, and about myself. I had a skill and others shined as a result; their hugs and gratitude gave me validation. In each session, I helped people escape for a little while into this magical place of glam, highlighting their best features. It was a chance to get playful and have fun. Wearing the clothes provided by the studio was like playing dress-up in a fashionable friend's closet. At that time the makeup was dark and bold since it would be lightened with soft- focus photography. The hair of the time was big, textured, and sprayed heavily to endure the outfit changes plus the hot lights in the studio. The confidence I saw in women of every size, age, and race helped me to understand something fundamental: Beauty can be found everywhere in everyone. It felt so special to be trusted in that vulnerable space by women I didn't know until that moment. Women have always been judged for being too sexy, too confident, too this or that, and in this space we encouraged people to be just exactly that, too much of whatever they wanted.

Because of my own insecurities and maybe even trauma, I knew, even at such a young age, that having someone trust me was a big honor. One of my favorite parts of the job was hyping up my clients to try an outfit or style that was out of their comfort zone, then focusing on their best features and confirming it by showing them their photos a week or so later. More often than not, the women I spent all this time trying to convince to wear a certain item of clothing, or try a new hairstyle, would come in to pick up their photos and be moved to tears by what they saw. They felt empowered, beautiful, and brave. I would be moved to tears, too, because something important was taking root in me every time this happened. My takeaway from my time working in this studio was that we all wanted to feel beautiful, seen, and celebrated. This was my introduction and the foundation to seeing the inclusive world I wanted to be a part of, where all were welcome to shine, including me.

Sadly, the mall job came to an end when they closed the Tucson franchise just as I was graduating high school. At the same time, the social security check I received monthly from my father's unexpected passing was stopping too. I didn't allow myself to really feel the disappointment—I couldn't because I was in survival mode—and anyway, self-pity would have been a waste of time.

Jobless and about to lose my social security, I was faced with figuring out what was next. I'd been told I needed to go to college, because "playing dress-up at the mall wasn't a real job anyway," at least that's what I had been told by family and friends. How was I going to provide for my family? Everyone wanted to know, including me. And the even bigger and ominous question that loomed: What did I want to be? How did I want to show up in the world? The teen-mom program I was in helped me with resources like early child development and parenting classes; they also helped find resources such as "Youth on Their Own," a nonprofit helping homeless teens or teens living on their own find college scholarships. I was a prideful person, and asking for help was hard for me; I didn't want to be perceived as needing a handout. But the very real truth was that I was living in a crappy, single-wide trailer with my son and boyfriend. I needed help, I needed mentorship. I needed someone to guide me through the next set of options.

This program determined that any minor who should still be in the home of a guardian but was living independently, without support, qualified for their services. And so with that, I was officially college-bound, entering on the promise of grants and scholarships that required a good GPA. With the help of "Youth on Their Own" and other financial aid, I put my love of glam to the side. Everyone around me kept emphasizing the message that beauty wasn't a real job or could never become a respectable career. Everywhere I turned, the feedback was the same:

You're a bright girl!

The beauty industry is for people who can't make it in school!

It's a superficial industry! Surely there is something more professional you could do.

I had little self-confidence without a makeup brush in my hand and initially bought into the narrative that there wasn't a professional future in the world of beauty. I let it go, which caused me to feel a sense of tremendous loss and deep grief. There were a couple subjects I liked in school and so I hoped I could find a new direction that offered the same level of joy. I was motivated to keep going in life and become a success because I had that sweet boy to provide for, and I was committed to him having everything he needed. When I was eighteen, the most available professional options for women were to become a nurse or a teacher. I loved working with children, so teaching became the most obvious choice. While attending college and working toward a degree in education, I was doing freelance weddings, proms, and editorial hair and makeup for magazines on the side. Sure, the extra money was much needed, but I really did it because I loved it.

I married my high school boyfriend and we planned for a second child immediately after the wedding. I knew this would sidetrack me from my professional goals for a bit, but I believed it would be worth it and maybe even fix us. We had been together for a few years and it seemed like the natural next steps, especially because we had already been living together. Get married. Have another kid. This was the proper order, despite my young age, I told myself.

The marriage was heading toward its end before we even reached our second anniversary, and we ended up in couple's therapy. I realized over time that while I had not picked a partner who screamed at me, hit me, or struggled with addiction like I had witnessed growing up, I had married a manipulator and a cheater. Not all of this was a shock, there was plenty of evidence along the way and I stayed. Once we were married, there were more clues and the inevitable fall outs continued. Go figure, another baby and a wedding didn't magically fix things.

I would ultimately continue to forgive him so we could still move forward with our relationship. Then, there was a light that clicked after one particular lie, and I realized I deserved real love and respect. For the first time I felt bold enough to not be afraid of being alone, and so I acted swiftly. It was like the blinders had come off, and I could see clearly that this wasn't loving behavior toward me. It was time to start loving myself. I realized how important it was to me that my children were proud of me; I wanted to be an example of the kind of woman they might marry or be someday, and that wasn't going to happen by staying in an unhealthy relationship. I didn't want to be like the women I watched growing up, who stayed at the cost of themselves or their children's safety and happiness. I took notice of the unspoken lesson taught from those around me; it was inferred that it was better to stay in an unhealthy relationship, than to be alone. But regardless, I knew it was time to take the road untraveled. I made a new vow, for my children and for myself; there would be no settling for anything less than great! Rather than find a way forward as a couple, therapy for me was a way to end the marriage smoothly and find a peaceful way to co-parent our two children under the age of five.

Although I had limited experience in therapy, I knew quickly this therapist was not a great fit. I could see her falling for the same thing I did, my charming ex-husband who was great with words. She was sensitive to his pain, he would cry, plead his desire to hold our marriage together while I was direct, no tears, and had no plan to continue the relationship. I had empathy for his pain, but was angry because no one was acknowledging mine. The therapist asked me hard questions, even prescribing me an antidepressant, and it seemed to me, she was guiding me to stay in the relationship for the children. For the first time in my life, I was being honest, and letting myself feel my feelings. I ultimately decided not to take the meds because I didn't want to be numbed out—I wanted to feel. So much of my life up until that point required me to hold in my feelings. This release was years in the making. I felt protective over the family I had made, and so I didn't share every lie or injustice to validate my decision to leave. I just made it clear that I was leaving for myself and my children. My hyperfocus on leaving wouldn't be swayed by the therapist, and looking back, I wonder if maybe that's the part she didn't like; that I couldn't be influenced. I was on a mission to exit this mess we made. We did a handful of sessions and I remember arriving at her office with a feeling that I was going into battle, not just with him but with her too. I would put on the metaphorical armor and go in to hold my position. In spite of her taking sides, I will always give her credit for the advice that changed my life course. She shared that time passes regardless of what you do. In a year's time, you are either a little tired and one step closer to your goal or well-rested and still have a long way to go. With that advice, I decided to quit college, became a single parent, and signed up for beauty school; I'd be tired, but I'd be one step closer to my dream. Even in my exhausted state, I could picture a future where I was safe, in every way; physically, mentally, and with a chance to define my future and live in peace with my children. No more wasting energy toward second-guessing myself in the relationship, no more doubting my worth, or worrying about his words and actions matching. I could now only focus on the kids and their needs. I knew things were about to get really tight financially, that divorce didn't mean my ex and I would all of sudden have a healthy co-parenting relationship, but I didn't care, because I had this deep feeling of trust in this new path. My eyes were open and I was ready for the new struggle of independence.

*   *   *

"A woman who cuts her hair is a woman who is about to change her life," Coco Chanel once said. I couldn't agree more, and so in the spirit of my newfound life-changing independence, I cut off my long dark locks. They represented bondage to me. Growing up in a house where I couldn't creatively express myself through hair or style and then gathering the courage to extricate myself from an unhealthy marriage that had kept me under lock and key, I found such power in cutting all my hair off. It declared to the world at large: "I am in control now." Like the Janet Jackson song. And it was

just the beginning of me finding my voice, and ultimately understanding the important role hair played
in my creative expression, identity, and power.

Looking back, it wasn't the most flattering
haircut, but it was in style and considered edgy. I
wore the back messy in super shortspikes, despite
my waves. I left the bangs, keeping the front a little
longer and played a lot with hair color. The back was
a darker color while the longer front pieces had some

well-placed chunky blonde pieces. This haircut is now referred to as "The Kate Plus Eight," but I will
say, I had it before she did! The feedback on my new look was unkind, but I didn't care.

With my divorce in process, and sporting my new power haircut, I felt more confident than I
had ever felt in my life when I started beauty school. I went in ready to pass all my courses (or maybe
even be asked to teach them!). The joke was on me, as it turns out, because being published in a
magazine or styling beautiful hair for a photoshoot or wedding did not qualify me for any special
treatment. It was so much harder than I expected. I felt like I had entered nursing school, as I spent
hours pouring over textbooks learning about the circulatory system and how to recognize diseases
and disorders in order not to spread them during services. It was clear: Health and sanitation is the
foundation of working in beauty, as much as doing good design work is. We spent so much time
learning basic chemistry and the pH scale to understand how to formulate hair color and understand
how it performs. I enjoyed science in school so that was helpful here, but even still, the complexity of
hair color and other chemical hair treatments still blows my mind today. There was so much science
and safety, and I grew frustrated because all I really wanted to know was: When can I do the hair?

Finally, it was time to get out of the classroom to learn how to hold a comb and scissors at the same time without cutting ourselves or a client (it's harder than you might think, still!). My beauty school teachers gave me the introduction in learning how to listen to the things my clients weren't saying. For instance, did their reference pictures and concerns about their hair or maintenance align? Asking questions to clarify their goals, managing expectations, and the importance of understanding good communication were all a part of my education. While they taught us basic haircuts and chemical applications, I soon discovered my experience with animals came in handy here too. I knew how to look at body language and trust my gut to ask more questions if the cues were off.

I had two young kids at home at this time; one had started kindergarten and the other one was still in daycare. I was working part-time at the front desk of a chain salon and doing hair on the side to make a little extra money. I was also trying to figure out how to be single while managing a life that was really beyond my twenty-three years. It was on a rare night out when this fragile game of real-life Jenga I was playing nearly came crashing down.

In the middle of my required hours for beauty school, I was on a much-needed night out when a friend and her boyfriend had an argument. We were standing outside of a bar when it happened, and I stepped in to confront him. He shoved me out of the way, which resulted in me falling and breaking my wrist. The layers of complication were unimaginable. The pain, the impact on my friendship with her, the fear of the impact of a broken wrist on my schooling and being able to take care of my kids with only one useful arm . . . all of those fears came to fruition when I was told by my orthopedic doctor to find another career path. I had three surgeries over the course of one year, resulting in wearing a cast for over six months. This kept me from doing hair. It wouldn't be the first time I was told I might not be able to do hair; and it wouldn't be the last time I would have to find a way to push through.

After my wrist had healed well enough for me to return to school, I learned that all my teachers had been fired and our school was under new ownership. I had originally picked this special school because I felt these teachers weren't washed up beauty pros but people with actual talent who currently worked in the field. We students, the clients, demanded answers from the new ownership. As a very prideful young person who did not possess the capability of backing down at this stage, I used my newly acquired voice to publicly declare an intention: I was now going to transfer to the other beauty school in town, their competitor. And so, I had to follow through. Two beauty schools and a hefty 1,600 required hours of work later, I was done. School was wrapped up, the state-board test was scheduled, and it was time to look for full-time work.

After I left with what was the equivalent of a bachelor's degree, I wanted more. It was time to get my master's by joining an apprenticeship. There was a big salon in my hometown, Gadabout Salon and Spas, where all the pretty gals and guys worked. I didn't overthink it, I just walked in and applied. Just like the mall job in high school, I knew if they gave me a chance and support, I had the determination to succeed. I felt imposter syndrome mounting as I filled out the application, but I knew I had to work alongside the best to become the best—and I knew this career was my destiny. This salon and spa was considered "high end," an overused term in the beauty industry now, and a phrase that really just means fancy and expensive. But they did offer great services in a modern environment, giving off a very cool vibe.

After almost two years of beauty school, and in my early twenties at this point, I committed another eighteen months to my training by accepting the position as an apprentice. This position meant I would be interning in the salon, and I would participate in an intense continuing education curriculum. My role in my day-to-day tasks was to help stylists manage the flow of their days by washing hair, sweeping up hair, and keeping things clean and stocked. If you were lucky enough to be seen as a hard worker, you could be asked to be a personal assistant to a senior stylist, someone who did a high volume of clients and was a high earner. I was lucky enough to be picked by one of the salon managers after a few months of being at the company, which meant I would work her hours and be her shadow. I was excited for the opportunity because I really respected Judy. Not only because she had a large clientele and did beautiful hair, but also because she was a former single mom who owned her own home and held a leadership role in a successful company. I was unknowingly desperate to see this example, and looked forward to learning from her personally and professionally. I also liked the idea of one-on-one support and not being pulled in so many different directions while taking instructions from stylists who have so many preferences on how they work.

The continuing education of my apprenticeship involved a variety of classes and required me to find models to practice what I was learning in exchange for brutally honest feedback. It is a vulnerable thing to create something you are proud of and also have the opportunity to be graded, but not always celebrated, in your efforts. This level of critique was far more intense than the level of scrutiny I received at beauty school; they commented on how I held the hair while cutting and made sure I understood why the elevation was integral to how my finished work in the style looked. I did get glimpses of the high I felt from working at Glamour Shots, and those moments carried me through the hard days. When I think back to this time, I often wonder if it was a combination of my generation and the house I grew up in that enabled me to make it through this trying ordeal. There wasn't a lot of positive affirmation or feedback flying around at my house, so I had to learn how to deal with criticism as a coping mechanism. Growing up, negative feedback felt like a reflection of me as a whole person, not just about that specific topic in question. Even after all these years, this can still flare up for me. I had to learn to fill my own cup up with positive thoughts and feelings about myself since I didn't have those voices of loved ones in my head doing it for me.

I figured a three-to-four-year investment to be a hairstylist and the opportunity for the life I wanted was worth it. I had hope, some validation from mentors, and a deep belief that this is where I belonged. And finally, I was starting to feel like I could fit in at the salon and in the industry. I was pleasantly surprised that this world of beauty, while at times feeling very superficial, was also a very kind and encouraging environment to be in. I met mentors who opened my mind through watching how they worked and played, this taught me how to dream bigger for myself. These people showed me how to give back to my community using my talents, how to enjoy travel, and make beautiful art. I made great friends and was supported as a single mom, helping with pickup or attending their sports to cheer them on. Almost thirty years later, I am still grateful for the strong foundation of hairstyling and the high bar I set for my career as a result of my foundation I received at Gadabout.

One of the most important lessons I have learned on this journey is that there is more than one way to be smart. This journey allowed me to meet so many smart people and alternate versions of intelligence—some were street smart, others financially savvy. There were the ones who possessed the coveted book smarts, but were flanked by the emotionally intelligent who were also great communicators. All these people showed me that intelligence isn't reserved for a select few; it is for those who have access and support to nurture it. I have leaned into my acceptance of my own intelligence; I am an artist, and this journey has also allowed me to define and explore my own version of feminism and beauty. More than anything, I know for a fact that I do fit into this world of beauty. That tomboy who would rather be on a horse or playing at the park or the girl who loved playing Barbie with her sister, who later learned to embrace both expressions of comfy and glam, would sure be proud of how far we have come. The grit and determination I have had until recently I thought was only fueled by being a role model for my children, or maybe proving myself for them, or even proving the world wrong. When actually, in fact this whole time, I was doing it for all the versions of me, to prove to me

I was worth this life I fought so hard to create. While my family and the example I am will always be a motivator, I am so glad I learned I was worth it too.

What has been the most unexpected lesson in your career?

"The variety of elements you must grow in and be good at to be successful. How to read people and understand different personality styles, as well as manipulate your personality to accommodate a variety of people. As a hairdresser, you must be friendly, polite, courteous, and helpful. Consistently. You must match their energy and meet their expectations to gain clientele. The salon team and philosophy carve and shape your behavior. In return, it molds a clientele—the consistency of your attitude, level of work, and behavior, along with attendance, is what maintains your clientele."

—SUSIE POWERS, Seattle, Washington
Thirty-five years in the industry

"Working in the beauty industry taught me that self-care is vital before taking care of others. In an industry where so much of your energy is devoted to others, it's essential to listen to your body's needs as you would listen to your client's goals in a consultation. It's easy to overlook your own needs in such a fast-paced environment, but it ultimately comes at a cost in the form of burnout, loss of inspiration or poor health. Through practicing intentional listening, you can sustain longevity in your health, relationships and career."

—MADISON GRIFFIN
Seven years in the industry

"BOUNDARIES!!! I feel a lot of us (hairstylists) tend to be people pleasers and caregivers, hence going into a service industry. When you're new to the industry, you're so eager to build a clientele that boundaries can fall to the wayside (if you've been lucky enough to be taught and introduced to boundaries). Growing into this business brings forth your own healing journey of learning how to set healthy boundaries in your business to prevent burn out and resentment toward your clients and your career. I've been learning and enforcing boundaries now, but it is an ever-learning practice that takes just that—years of practice and knowing that it won't all fall apart because you have healthy boundaries and aren't jumping to say yes to everything and everyone."

—MARIAH SMILEY, Ann Arbor, Michigan
Eighteen years in the industry

"The most unexpected lesson in my career is there hasn't been a clear road map. I had to learn and truly understand that not everyone's journey to the same goal will look the same. Yes, there are similarities, but no one's looks the same. For example, there are plenty of educators in the industry; however, we did not all start the same way into becoming an educator. Some trained under someone, others maybe auditioned to be an educator with a brand, and then some were discovered. It's not a very clear road map. I think the thing that we have to truly understand is that you just have to stay consistent with your plan to get to your goal."

—BRENDNETTA ASHLEY, California
Twenty-one years in the industry

"Grace. For you and others. It's very hard to wear all the hats you need to wear as a stylist, owner, artist, and human being. You can't do it all perfectly all the time. Let that go. Give people grace as often as you can, and remember to give it to yourself as well."

—ALEXIS ROBINSON, Seattle, Washington
Over twenty years in the industry

"The most unexpected lesson in my career has been the critical importance of thorough due diligence before investing in education or new partnerships in the education world. In today's saturated market, there's an abundance of companies and educators vying for attention. What I've found to be paramount when considering further education is to actively seek referrals from stylists within my specific geographic area who have demonstrably succeeded with the company or educator I'm researching.

It's crucial to ensure that the education provided is tailored to my unique demographic and location. What might work in one region or for a different client base may not be applicable to my specific situation. By focusing on local success stories, I can confidently invest in education that truly adds tangible value and is relevant to the real-world scenarios I encounter in my salon business.

—DELORA MAY DAY, Columbia, Missouri
Sixteen years in the industry

A PAGE FOR YOUR THOUGHTS

CHAPTER 2

THERE ARE SO MANY WAYS
YOU CAN DO HAIR

Pixie Cut: A *pixie cut* is a versatile short hairstyle, generally short on the back and sides of the head and slightly longer on the top, with very short bangs. It is a variant of a crop. It can be styled soft, feminine or with a lot of texture and an edge.

The pixie cut was first popularized in the 1950s when Audrey Hepburn wore the style in the 1953 movie Roman Holiday. "Hepburn went a long way to making short hair mainstream and got a lot of credit for popularizing the pixie cut," explains hair historian Rachael Gibson.

Like a pixie cut, my career has been edgy, soft, feminine.

HOW TO FIND A PATH

I have reinvented myself many times throughout my career. These changes have been motivated by various reasons; from needing extra income or needing more creative variety—whatever the reason, it has always led to using reinvention as a tool for growth.

It has always been exciting to experiment with the many ways I could use my license and skills. Before entering the beauty industry, one of my interests was education and the idea of teaching in beauty was definitely a path I wanted to explore. I think it's safe to say that, for a while, I was a bit of a workaholic while trying on all the ways I could create. I loved feeling like I added value, being on a team and contributing my art, and staying busy; it helped give me a healthy outlet during personal low moments. Getting involved in opportunities beyond the day-to-day salon life also helped me fill my downtime when my kids weren't with me. My growth journey, personally and professionally, hasn't been linear, and it has not always trended upward. It has felt more like a roller coaster to me, extreme highs and the lowest of lows.

I have always been a planner, overthinker, and list maker. I try on multiple scenarios and possible outcomes of choices, I have learned this is probably a trauma response, a sense of security or safety I try to create for myself when things feel out of control. Even if maladaptive, this strategy has helped me prepare for what *might happen*, which has allowed me not to be paralyzed by shock or fear when situations fall apart. Being prepared in this way allows me to take action swiftly. One specific strategy I use consistently is to create formulas of operation. For example, when I have a big idea, I often start at the end, identifying my desired outcome, and then consider the steps that will help me reach my goal. My process requires me to be as specific as I can be all the way to the final result. Big ideas are the easy part for me; I challenge myself to think expansively. I've used this formula to help me decide where to live, or who I wanted to surround myself with, and the lifestyle I wanted to create and maintain. I think about my ideal clients, how it feels going to work, and what I want in order to balance that life I have imagined. Once I have created the vision of what success looks like, I work backward and create a map for how to get there.

Goal setting for the future requires a willingness to do things I have not attempted before, while along the way embracing a practice of flexibility. All goals require small, consistent actions. Like a diet, or a healthy lifestyle change, going to the gym once doesn't get you in shape or increase your strength, nor does eating one healthy meal get you to your ideal weight or health outcome. Many people throughout my life talked about their big plans, but I never saw them execute them, nor did they ever share their small steps, nor did I see the consistent small actions. Time will continue to pass regardless of whether we take steps forward, but it's the consistency of doing something that turns a goal into reality. The actions and effort is the difference between the dreamers and the doers. I realized I did not want to be the person who was talking about the same dream for ten or even twenty years like some of my peers, mine was to move.

I grew up in Tucson, I learned the longer you stay anywhere the smaller it becomes. Sure, it could make for a fun childhood, and it was definitely a great college town, but I quickly noticed the in-between phase, postcollege to retirement, was lacking in opportunities. A lot of my friends and I talked about leaving our town in search of something different, many didn't make a plan or ever move. I no longer wanted to be the person complaining about my hometown and wanted to really explore what it would take to leave.

As I prepared for my move, I learned I could redefine the meaning of many words; the most significant being failure and regret. For me, failure is *not* trying something I can't stop thinking about, regardless of the outcome. Like choosing to be a single parent, starting my career in beauty, leaving college, and uprooting my family to Seattle. I understood, over time, that the effort wasn't wasted even if the outcome was not what I desired; it wasn't a failure if it all didn't work out the way I had envisioned, but rather, it was information. I can honestly say, I have never regretted the things I tried, even the jobs that didn't work out, or the people that didn't work out either. I have experienced regret when I didn't say the things I needed to say or set the boundary that needed to be set, which I continue to work on. Doing what scares me, while believing in the journey, is a reminder that more than one thing can be true.

*   *   *

I learned early on in my career that freelance work, although exciting and rewarding, didn't create enough consistent opportunities in my area to make a living. I was extremely focused on finding my place in beauty and wanted to create ways to use all my experiences. I loved competing. The salon I worked at was supportive of my journey, from creating behind the chair to participating in competitions to completing ongoing education. I entered creative competitions at school in order to test my skills against other stylists. The competitions weren't just about winning for me; it was about the validation I received from my peers, the judges, and knowing that I performed better than I had previously performed. Over time, I needed less validation from others and measured success by how much I loved what I was doing and how my individual work improved.

I have been asked throughout my career, and I have overheard so many clients ask other stylists, "What else do you want to be other than a stylist? " For some of my friends, they have been very content working behind the chair, taking classes to remain relevant, and have no desire for more responsibility in regards to work or leadership roles. That is the wonderful thing about the industry, you can be a career stylist, or one can do many other things in addition to that, or pivot completely leaving the salon life using skills that have been acquired over time. Not all of the things I've done were motivated by money; there were other exchanges of energy that were just as important to me, like how it felt to share my time and talents when working on a creative project to make something beautiful without rules and to give opportunities to others to showcase their work.

I've held various roles in beauty and this winding path has ultimately landed me in what I define as success: A woman with financial independence who can travel and have plenty of time with her loved ones, with enough leftover to explore a healing journey through therapy and coaching too.

EVERYONE'S GOTTA START SOMEWHERE

Hair and makeup at Glamour Shots in the mall was my introduction into this world, and it hooked me. I have some friends in beauty who started their careers at makeup counters at the mall, worked as support staff at salons then went to beauty school to become an esthetician or hairstylist after they were hooked. I know working at Sally's Beauty Supply or Ulta was the intro some needed to get into the industry as well. No matter how you were introduced, I do recommend anyone considering a career in beauty to try it on before committing! I refer to it as speed dating; find a job that lets you peek behind the curtain to see what it really takes, meet the people who have been in it for a while, ask questions you have about the field, and get real answers. This allows you to make an informed decision before committing to the cost of schooling and the time investment needed.

I like the quote from Glennon Doyle: "Stop asking people for directions to a place they have never been." Although she is talking about deep life stuff, it applies in any situation. You may have a similar situation to mine, and your friends and family might not be so encouraging as you explore this industry. But the truth is they have probably never been there before, so go find out for yourself if it is for you and find the people who have been where you are hoping to go. Ask them your questions. Listen to their advice. Get yourself out of your comfort zone and ask them for a copy of their map. Their way isn't the only way, but it will help to see which turns and detours they have taken as you begin to navigate your own path toward success.

IT'S ALL IN WHO YOU KNOW!

I took the skills I learned from Glamour Shots and used them to go find work as a freelance hair and makeup artist once Glamour Shots closed. I was able to create a side hustle that allowed me to earn some money doing editorial work which led to my work being published in magazines, igniting my love for collaborating with photographers and seeing my work as art. I also did wedding hair and makeup, plus other special occasion styling such as for proms. The opportunities began when I just started talking to people I knew, making sure my community was aware I had a kit and a skill set. For example, if you get one gal for prom hair and makeup, it's really easy to let her know you could take up to four of her friends and turn it into a group experience. These groups of high schoolers would give me two years of repeat business for dances, and oftentimes, they would refer me to their underclass friends. Their mothers would also use me from time to time for special occasions. I was at an age where people around me were getting married, this was another opportunity. Similarly I would let them know how many people I could accommodate, once the relationships were established within the bridal party, that would lead to more opportunities as the others got married or had special occasions. This is how I came to meet a variety of photographers, wedding planners, and others who became a great source of referrals. I did good work, showed up on time, and was professional as I worked in homes and hotels. Before I knew it, I was turning down work. Finding a group of professionals that offer skills that are complementary to yours is a great way to create a referral network. Creatives supporting each other is a tried and true way to increase opportunities.

A word of caution: Pay attention to the reputations of the people you align yourself with professionally as you will become a reflection of them. Are they honest, professional, do they create a safe space, reliable; does their art align with work you are proud of, and do they treat people in a way in which you align?

SALON LIFE 101

I was a receptionist at a chain salon while attending beauty school, which really became my intro to learning about the inner workings of a salon. From how to book clients to the importance of customer service and first impressions to welcoming clients into a space, I started to understand value, and why people decide to spend their time and money somewhere and what entices them to come back. In the '80s movie Pretty Woman, there's a scene when Julia Roberts is turned away by a snobby shop keeper on Rodeo Drive because she is not their usual clientele. Something in me resonates with the last part of that scene when she stops by with her multitudes of shopping bags from designer stores and with a triumphant smile mocks them with her words while saying, "Big mistake!" Customer service starts with welcoming people, no matter how they are dressed or how their hair is done, and without making any assumptions about their income level. The service, how they feel during it, and your consistency as a service provider will be what brings people back.

All of these things add up when people measure value. Did you respect their time by starting the appointment on time? Did you apologize or let them know ahead of time if you were running late? Are you gossiping about previous clients or with your co-workers during their visit? Do you look professional and ready to work or are you tired from a late night out and distracted by drama? Are your tools and station clean and inviting? With the amount of access to reality shows and social media, the public is more aware than ever about a standard of cleanliness expected in this type of setting. And this is all before you even start the service!

Once they are in your chair, it's time to consult with them. Ask yourself: Are you open to hearing that things didn't work out last time or that they want to change it up? Do you provide a collaborative and safe space for people to be honest and vulnerable? Does what you promised match the end result and ultimately how they feel about the experience beyond how they look? Value is a collection of it all. Consider going out for dinner, expecting the best meal of your life but the service was horribly slow, your fork was dirty, and your water glass had lipstick on the rim—and it wasn't yours. You might give it one more chance, thinking it was an off night, but probably wouldn't give it more than that. It's the same thing with your client. You might get a second chance at a first impression, but probably not a whole lot more.

How long have you been with your stylist and why do you stay with them?

"I believe it has been like eleven years. I stay because she does an amazing job, listens to what I would like done, and is fun to talk with while I am there getting my hair done."

—SHANNON D.
Seattle, Washington

"Annie has been my friend, therapist, confidant, hype girl, and stylist for over twenty years. We met back in high school in Tucson, and honestly, I tell people I moved to Seattle because my hair stylist was here—and I'm only half joking!

I stay with Annie because she's a total wizard with my hair, which is no small feat—many, many people have tried and failed. I trust her completely. If I walk in saying, "I want bangs," Annie knows me well enough to laugh and say, 'Gurrrl— Let's try clip-ins first, and I'll dye them so you don't have regrets.'

That's the kind of trust we have—she gets me. Beyond her skills, she's one of the most kind-hearted and genuine people I know. She's my people, and I wouldn't go anywhere else.

It's all about the trust."

—LEAH O.
Seattle, Washington

"I have been with Annie since 2007. I stay with her because of multiple reasons. The first reason being that I feel like it is truly more than a haircut when I see her. We catch up and get to know what's happened over the last few months, reminiscing on different moments and life events. It truly feels like Annie has watched me grow up. I feel seen with her. I also stay with her because I can tell she has a true passion for her work. She takes the time to get to know what I want while providing honest feedback and giving me direction on what would look best. Annie also takes the time to continue learning. As a teacher this is very impressive and appealing to me! I admire someone with her drive who is never done educating herself. Finally, Annie is someone I look forward to seeing. Every time I get my hair done by her, I know I am going to feel and look special that day."

—MEGAN R.
Seattle, Washington

"I've been with Annie for over fifteen years. She has been with me through my most important seasons of life (dating, marriage, building a career, becoming a mother, rebuilding a career after becoming a mother, loss of family and friends, tough relationships, and every holiday and random Tuesday in between ;)) I find she is more of a therapist than hairstylist. She's also a close family friend, mentor, and someone I look up to in business and life. I have learned from her it's so much more than hair—it's a reflection of how we feel and are doing inside. She helps guide me when I want to make rash decisions (with my hair—and also, life) because wouldn't you know the two go hand in hand more than one thinks (or maybe the hair stylists all know this universal truth;)). I stay with Annie because the relationship is one built on trust and time. She's also very funny, smart, and always uplifting, even when I know it's been a hard week or month for her. She's selfless in a way I think all great people in client services come to be. Lastly, she shows up for me in my personal life."

—ASHLYN P.
Seattle, Washington

"I have been with my stylist for nineteen years. You can assume, from that length of time, that she's a supremely skilled stylist, and she is—I've never NOT absolutely loved my hair. But it's her warmth, her wit, her generosity, her empathy, and her intelligence that has me bound to her for life. I learn something from her every visit, I laugh very hard with her every visit, and I always leave looking and feeling MUCH better than when I walked in. I now live 1,200 miles away and she's one of the people I miss, and someone I still fly up to see to make me laugh, to teach me things, to listen and yup—to do my hair. I feel like I'm my best self: I'm put together. I'm confident. I feel younger. And I feel very, very lucky to have this woman on my team."

—KIRA K.
Tucson, Arizona

WANT TO BE A CAREER STYLIST? GET YOUR MASTERS

I joined an apprenticeship in a salon after graduation, and this was the foundation to my career. I call this getting your masters. In my opinion, beauty school alone or interning (working in a salon as an assistant without a structured curriculum) doesn't prepare you for taking clients and creating long-term success as a career-minded stylist. An apprenticeship program is a structured program that will support your growth through education and accountability. This prepares you for becoming a career stylist, and then getting on the floor to take your own clients, which is such a rewarding milestone to make. It is important, when looking for a salon, to understand their definition of interning or an apprenticeship, so you are making the correct choice that aligns with your goals. My program was a year and a half, depending on the salon and the areas of focus. Are you only offering haircuts or chemical services or can everything impact the length of the program? A paid position in the right salon environment allows you to start building relationships with clients so when you go on the floor to take clients, you are a familiar face and the salon can support building your clientele.

BECOME A TEACHER

I became a color educator for the brand Framesi, which we were using at the salon. The benefit of working for a large corporate salon and them having a great relationship with the brand, and this helped me start my process. FYI, no matter how big or small the salon you work in is, you can apply to work for a brand.

Becoming certified as an educator with Framesi had many positive side effects: I was able to teach outside of my salon for additional income, I got to be part of a group of people who loved hair and learning, and I was able to teach in my salon and became a better colorist because I had a deeper understanding of how the chemicals performed, achieving more consistent outcomes. If you are

in a suite working alone, being an educator can be a great way to build community, expand your personal branding, identify yourself in your market as an educator, and sharpen your skills. My clients loved hearing that I was continuing my education and teaching other stylists; it led to more referrals from my clients. This also honored that part of me who started school to become an educator because of my desire to teach. I love sharing what I have learned, and if I found a hack, I was happy to pass it along to others. Gatekeeping what I learned was never my vibe, no matter how much you share what you know, no one will ever be you. It is so great to take the lessons of others and put your spin on it.

A NEED FOR OTHER OUTLETS

I was invited to join the creative design team for my salon. This was such an honor and reunited me with the love of seeing my work in print. I personally needed a range of creative expressions to feel fulfilled, and still do. I love creating beautiful hair for clients, and I love creating abstract looks that you wouldn't see walking down the street on a regular Monday morning. Being on this team meant a group of us would create collections for the changing seasons, and we were forecasting new trends, doing them on models, and having professional photos taken for marketing, in the name of salon education. We would run ads at the

local university for a model call or hire talent from the local agencies, then partner with boutiques to dress our models. This team would spend time together researching previous trends in hair, fashion, and makeup. It was a great way to continue editorial work, with my salon's support, and we would enter our images into competitions.

No matter the size of your salon or how big your budget is, you can put together a team or you alone could start a creative project. You can use existing clients or do a model call on your social media that advertises they get free hair services, but be clear on the looks you are wanting to create. Find a photographer and makeup artist who might be willing to do some trading of services with you, or who desires to build their portfolio for a social media content collaboration. It has to be said that with our current technology, your phone and some editing apps can go a long way in getting started too.

MOVING STATES

Boldly, I moved states and started over with no clients in a commission-only salon. Leaving a full book of clients after working about seven years was a crazy idea to most people I knew. But I knew if I didn't make the leap right then, I never would. I was getting more and more comfortable in my position at the salon and in my life in general, and I knew that if I was going to start over, I should do it while I still remembered how to. I did lots of research on cities, weather, schools for my kids, and salon opportunities. I picked Seattle because I knew I needed to be watered, literally. After a lifetime spent in the desert, I needed

seasons and to be near natural beauty. Moving to Seattle would keep me on the West Coast, offering easier access to family, which was a consideration.

I visited Seattle for the first time in early November; it was gray and moody, which matched my vibe perfectly at that time. I had also read it was astrologically a Scorpio town. I didn't know what that meant other than I was a Scorpio and I was looking for any sign of confirmation I was making the right move. It checked a lot of boxes: a lush green place, four seasons, plenty of salons, and an environment where growth was embraced.

BALANCING IT ALL

There were times when my identity as a creative was in conflict with the other ways that I needed to show up in my life. I learned at an early age that our priorities change, and sometimes we must recalibrate in an effort to maintain our joy while making a living. This inspired some of my salon moves in Seattle, as well as the relationships, personally or professionally, I worked at or let atrophy.

Before moving, I struggled at times with measuring my worth by how productive I was, and not allowing time for rest; the glorification of busyness. The purpose of this move was to recalibrate my values and reflect on who I wanted to be in this next chapter of my story. I had learned that seeking a work-life "balance" left me feeling like a failure as a single mom of two kids at times and a failure at my career occasionally because I was simply outnumbered. One of my personal goals was to create a life that allowed me to show up as the mom I wanted to be, cheering on my kids during their activities, and being able to connect with them in the mornings before school. I was motivated to be home for homework and bedtime more nights than not. I wanted to be kinder and more patient with them and with myself while creating memories we could reflect on later in life. They were at the age of remembering these years, and I knew the impact it could have later as I reflected on my own childhood. Plus, I didn't want to remember just the stress, but rather, the joy. Being a workaholic early in my career didn't serve my family, but it did serve my ego. When I made the move to Seattle, it was with the intention that I would focus on investing more time in all parts of my life, especially since I was choosing to live in a place I had no support system and the kids wouldn't be going to their dad's house for an overnighter. This new life required me to show up differently. I was ready for the chance to start over, again, and to choose us.

NEW CITY AND THE SAME GOAL: GROW!

I was still on mission to figure out how to get busy behind the chair by building relationships and finding ways to foster creative outlets. This is still how I was going to make a living. I was still an educator for Framesi so that allowed me to teach, earn a little income, and connect in my new community too. I joined a new salon that had some fresh ideas about a head-to-toe consultation. The owner had a med-spa practitioner, a wardrobe stylist, makeup artist, and someone from our hair team offering a very What Not to Wear inspired vibe. It was called a Spotlight appointment where we would all come around and offer our feedback on what services and styles were best for the client.

This new approach to building business was a success. We met with local politicians getting ready to run for office, stay-at-home moms reentering the workforce, and corporate gents and gals wanting to level up at their companies. This concept, and the owner's reputation in brow art, got the salon a lot of press, and I was able to gain some wonderful clients; some I still see after twenty years of being in Seattle and multiple salon moves.

This salon's press resulted in an opportunity to be a guest hair and makeup artist on the actual What Not to Wear when they did their Seattle episodes. I was fortunate to be picked for this by the salon owner because of my resume. Finding a salon that appreciated my experience while building their own brand allowed me to use a variety of my skills and build my client list at the same time. It offered opportunities for more creative projects and press features, as well as an invitation to compete in local hair competitions. This salon offered me a jump start into the culture of hair in a new city. Although it would only be my home for a year, I'm still grateful for the rapid-fire introduction to Seattle, and the many lasting industry friends and clients.

I left my salon in Arizona feeling like it was more of a family. This move taught me that most other professions don't consider their place of work family. For me, the definition of family was complicated and unhealthy, that first salon in Seattle mirrored some of that, and if I couldn't contribute to it changing, then I would choose to leave. So I did. Since, I look for a work environment that mirrors more of a championship sports team: a clear leader willing to do what is right even if it means you are disliked, and training and coaching with accountability and teamwork . . . not a dysfunctional family that asks you to be loyal in spite of the unwillingness to do better when something isn't working, or if there is a toxic culture. It isn't always easy to know what you are joining until you are in the fold. Unfortunately, this contributed to a few of my salon moves in my new city, but I had made enough personal and professional bold decisions to know not to stay in something that would cost me my peace or safety.

TIME TO CHANGE IT UP

After working as a commission stylist for three years, I had the opportunity to become an independent contractor and rent a booth, my fourth salon move in my new city. A friend I had made from the first salon I worked in had landed at a place that was growing, and she thought of me. After talking to the owner and understanding the opportunity to grow my books was really possible, I made the leap. This took a lot of research. I had to figure out how much it cost to provide the services I offered, how to order products and manage inventory, and since I would be responsible for my own health care, retirement, and paying my taxes, I had to learn the business of running a business. While feeling very overwhelmed by another learning curve, I also knew I had come this far and I was desperate to make this new city that my little family had fallen in love with work out. I was loving the new version of myself and my kids I was seeing as we were leaning on each other making this new life.

A SOLID FOUNDATION MAKES FOR A STRONG STRUCTURE

After spending five years in one location leasing a chair and growing a successful personal brand, it was time to consider my next professional move. I read books, took classes, and met with various small-business owners to learn how they had gotten started. I was on a quest to see if salon ownership could be my next thing. I spent countless hours googling local laws for having employees, how much commercial leases cost, how to write a business plan, salon design ideas, and how to hire commercial contractors. All that research led to writing a business plan, an employee manual, and creating a curriculum for an apprenticeship, all with opening my own salon in mind.

I had worked in a couple of great places that had these things clearly laid out, which provided a good reference. I watched many creative friends jump right into opening up a business with no plan only to end up going back to do these steps. I had a variety of experiences in a bunch of things in beauty but there are no shortcuts in learning something new. This new role of salon ownership would require me to do things I hadn't done before and with that, I had to be a version of myself I had never been before either.

MY SUCCESS FORMULA: CORE VALUE SYSTEM + PERSONAL AND FINANCIAL GOALS

My Core Values: To be a safe place and contribute to my family's goals. To show my kids a mother who loves herself and that is not afraid to express it to them or others. To have a healthy partnership that allows us to be the best versions of ourselves, challenging each other to grow while holding space. I operate from faith in the unseen while believing what is in front of me. To have fiercely fought for my kids to have opportunities I did not—and to continue to.

What are your core values today?

Early on in my life, I operated from a practice of living within my means, which for me meant deciding to no longer have credit cards. I couldn't juggle that responsibility and all the variables that came along with them. I knew my fixed costs, which were the nonnegotiables; the roof over our heads, transportation, childcare, and basic needs. I kept things simple for many years.

The next layer of financial responsibility was my kids extracurriculars and interests. These costs changed many times throughout the years as they aged and we moved. There were times I couldn't count on child support so that required me to take on more work. Quarterly check-ins on my operating household budget were needed for many years. Now we have yearly or mid-year check-ins depending on what's going on. My relationship with credit cards or lines of credit has changed too. Knowing your numbers to live, play, and save will keep you focused on your current priorities and setting goals for growth. Now as a business owner and commercial real estate owner, we do the same check-in yearly or mid-year on the operating budget and goals too.

Do you know your current household operating costs? Do you have a growth plan for your business to support the life you want to create?

I learned success requires you to check-in regularly to make sure you are operating from your definition. My numbers continue to change but my need to know them, and checking in on my core values, has not. Progress over perfection was a mantra as I worked on mastering my art and my budget. I have also worked hard to heal my scarcity mindset around money and live in an abundance mindset while finding contentment. It is so nice to feel genuine excitement for others as they travel or meet a financial goal without envy. I continue to live within my means and work toward the things that I dream of, which, at this stage, is mostly experiences with my loved ones.

What have you learned from your hairstylist?

"I am not even sure where to start when it comes to what I've learned from Annie! On the hair front, I've learned that you wear it every day so it's one of the best investments you can make to feel like your best self. I've also learned that summer is NOT the time to try a shorter cut when you have hair like mine. On the personal front, I've learned and been inspired by Annie on a very regular basis. It's been an honor to be with her from when she rented a chair at Swoop, to when she opened AFH Salon in Madison Valley, to when she bought her Capitol Hill space, and I've learned that you should always push to become better at your craft, make others around you better, give back, and chase your dreams, even (and especially!) when it feels like a very long haul."

—MAUREEN S.
Seattle, Washington

"I've learned to embrace my sparkly gray streak, the best products to use in my hair, how to style it, and also . . . all the best movies and TV shows to watch and the best places to travel and shop."

—SUZZANE M.
Seattle, Washington

CHAPTER 3

THERE'S MORE GROWING
HERE THAN JUST HAIR!

The Bob Cut: Also known as a *bob*. A short to medium length haircut, in which the hair is typically cut straight around the head at approximately jaw level, and no longer than shoulder-length.

This served as a symbolic departure from traditional gender roles and women having long hair. Fast forward to the twentieth century, the bob haircut's roots can be traced back to the 1910s–1920s when it emerged as a symbol of liberation and modernity.

This haircut and its many variations is a personal favorite to wear, I love growing my hair then getting a big dramatic chop.

HAIR WE GO

Most new clients, after a few minutes of being focused on the service part of the conversation, will inevitably ask me: "Why did you get into doing hair?"

Most stylists' answers will include some version of: I am a creative person, I love making people feel good about themselves, I could never work behind a desk, I am an artist, or maybe, I thought it would be easy.

It has been reported by schools that only 50 percent of those who finish beauty school actually end up making a career of it, some don't even get their license after completing all those hours. Some people never even actually end up working in the field, while others view it as a job, a short-term endeavor. Regardless of who enters this industry, long term or short, the reality is: This path can be physically, emotionally, and mentally hard. I've been working in beauty for almost thirty years. Many times throughout my career my why has changed: It started as a love for beauty and an opportunity to use the skills, for my interest in beauty to develop, and to gain financial security as I left my marriage. Then, over the years, it evolved into a passion for creating and a fire to leave a legacy beyond doing great hair and to hopefully inspire others along the way. The why can change, and for some it might not, but it is good to check in with yourself. Knowing my why helps me continue to show up when things are challenging. Why am I doing this? Why should I keep going?

LET'S GET PHYSICAL!

I've dealt with a frozen shoulder, or bursitis as it is medically termed. This is considered a repetitive use injury caused by body positioning. As a stylist we hold our arms in unnatural positions for extended periods of time. When we are applying color, or blow drying, or hunched over and twisted while shampooing a client's hair, our bodies are in uncomfortable positions for hours. I have recently learned, as I entered menopause, it's a common side effect of that too. A double whammy. Over the years, due to repeated exposure, I have developed a variety of sensitivities to products and hair color as well; sometimes products can cause a rash on my hands and arms that can be very itchy; the worst cases cause asthma flare ups too.

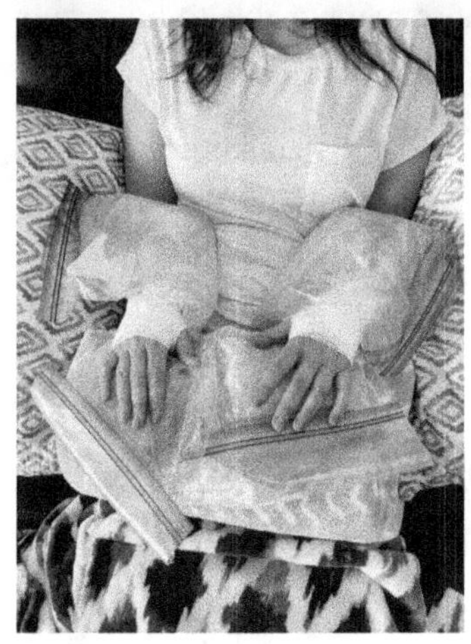

I had bilateral carpal tunnel surgery in 2022. The need for this surgery was also a result of repetitive use of certain muscles from haircutting, and the twisting and turning of a round brush for styling. Although I needed surgery on both hands, I wouldn't recommend doing it at the same time; I couldn't dress myself or even feed myself right after surgery. They did warn me about this, but I wanted the least amount of downtime possible, so I went for the double surgery. It was during this process that I was also diagnosed with arthritis in my right hand. The treatment for the arthritis was some occupational therapy, wearing a hand brace while I slept or at work during a flare up. My chiropractor will adjust my hand and I'll receive the occasional cortisone shot, so far that is two times a year. I do my best to eat well, move my body, and have recently added chiropractic visits and massage to my wellness routine in order to slow the progression, but at times, it still hurts horribly.

Most of us were told in school how important stretching is; taking care of your body is key if you want to have a long career in beauty, they said, and boy, they weren't kidding. Since I started in the industry at such a young age, understandably, I felt invincible. Hindsight, ever the truth illuminator, says to me often, "Girl, why didn't you do those stretches consistently?" From my experienced perspective now, I would say to anybody starting out in this industry, no matter their age, that it is extremely important to stretch and learn good posture and proper form when providing services. Maintaining physical health doesn't just include how one stands, or the repetitive nature of the job, it's about choosing the right tools.

Years ago, it wasn't acceptable to sit or use a step stool when working with a client. The weight of hair dryers and other tools has changed considerably too. It is now more manageable to hold your hand in a more neutral position for a longer period of time, and it is more acceptable to adjust your body to a position that works well for you, even if that means sitting or using a step stool. It's never too late (or too early) to invest in your physical fitness and overall health by practicing self-care through tool purchases and body adjustments.

NOW ON TO HOW IT FEELS

I'm of the generation of salon culture where we practiced the mantra "Act as if," or another way to phrase it: "Fake it until you make it." Act as if you're confident (even if your hands are shaking in your shears!); Act as if you're well-rested and ready (even though you spent ten hours at the salon and went to class after the night before, or maybe you had a late night to let off some steam or your kiddo couldn't sleep).

This is a commitment we as stylists make as we walk through the door. Like an actor stepping into character as they moved onto the set, I, too, would morph into another persona when walking into work. This mindset made sense to me; don't bring your baggage to work, be upbeat, and perform as a part of the modern zeitgeist of the '80s and '90s. I was very familiar with this type of performance because I grew up in a time and place where you did not talk about your struggles with others. I had mastered the art of acting okay from a very young age. Pretending I was safe, happy, and that I had it all together was as natural to me as my wavy unruly hair. While parts of me fought against this misrepresentation of reality, there was a part of me that understood why this demand came to be. I believe we are responsible for how we show up in the world, as well as the vibe we bring into a space. While I do subscribe to this ideology, I also feel that what's missing in this conversation is the fact that doing our best is a moving target every day. The odds of someone sitting in your chair and the conversation going from how many inches to cut off to sharing a deeply personal trauma with you is very high! It takes practice to hold space, not be reactive, and focus on your art when you've been triggered.

*   *   *

Early in my career, I hadn't done a lot of personal work and was unprepared when clients would become vulnerable with me when in my chair. I was pretty guarded in the early years, I shared only surface-level personal things that could connect me with a client, and if anything ever got too personal, I would quickly redirect the question back to them. Looking back, I can see this was a deeper level in learning the art of connection; what was sharing versus what was oversharing, and how to balance my nervousness about not being seen as a mess. Honestly, I am still working on this. After years of therapy and healing work, it's gotten much better, but it is still something that is always on my mind.

I've always prided myself in my consultations, asking specific questions to understand who somebody is, and to provide the best hairstyle that would work for their lifestyle. That was the easy part for me. The hard part? Understanding that the consultations I conducted were also potentially creating space for people to share some very vulnerable and sometimes heavy personal things. During an initial consultation, I've had a client break down in tears from a recent divorce—they came in with the need to reinvent. Or the client who comes in terrified after a disaster from their last hair service trauma. I am honored to be trusted with the raw vulnerability these clients come to me with. Sometimes, after people open up, they express shame and guilt for sharing. There will be much apologizing and embarrassment at the next appointment. Often, they even promise not to cry or be emotional again.

Another complicated layer at the time I entered the beauty industry was that society discouraged conversations about religion, belief systems, politics, and personal values in professional settings; we wouldn't want to offend our clients. The unspoken rule here was to be agreeable. When you have a client who says things that offend you unknowingly, states a prejudice or a bias against you or your family or your belief system, you can imagine how unprepared we were to deal with it since "Smile and change the subject!" was how we were coached. Over time, we as an industry have evolved, I know I sure have, by practicing not to be so agreeable. This requires us to heal our own traumas, take responsibility for how we show up, and learn how to set boundaries so the space is safe not just for our clients, but for ourselves. I've learned over the years that I'm not an agreeable servant but someone who provides a service. Now, I'm less about being agreeable, even while still triggered by certain topics, and more about holding space while setting boundaries. Most importantly, there is no tolerance for hate in my chair or salon.

There are plenty of times I can agree to disagree and sit in that potential discomfort while providing a service. By no means am I saying our differences or ignorance on a subject is all bad. I have learned so much about the beauty of other people's traditions, religions, and cultures through doing their hair. I try to stay curious without judgement. In what most others would consider a surface-level relationship, I have been exposed to a variety of viewpoints from people on environmental issues, disaster relief, inequality in education, and a variety of other social issues and local movements that have invited me to get involved in their activism.

THE COVID DAYS

I heard this said online, and it really spoke to me: "We were all weathering the same storm, but we were in different boats." I loved this when I read it; everyone's impact during the pandemic varied so much, even though they shared a similar experience. Some were rowing their own boats packed with family to safety through the storm, and some were on yachts outfitted with a full-service staff as they navigated the storm. As I worked and lived in Seattle, the range of my immediate community really reflected this. I definitely experienced financial fear, as I navigated all the relief options and did my best to understand the strings that came with them as a small business owner. My husband was able to switch to online and maintain his income, which was such a relief. As for me, the old adage of, "If you don't have a butt in the chair, you don't get paid," certainly applied.

This time deserves an asterisk; it changed me in ways that now I can be grateful for, but at the time, felt incredibly hard. I acknowledge that statement comes from a place of privilege. This time really sped up my learning curve on holding boundaries too. Getting still and comfortable with myself in the quiet in a way I had never chosen to do, was a gift. I am grateful to live in a city where the virus was treated seriously, and for the most part, our community supported each other, which helped with my own anxiety about getting sick. I was one of the people on the vulnerable list at that time, due to my asthma and other health issues. There were additional policies we were mandated to implement, like capacity limits, clients coming alone to their appointments, or masking inside. I felt prepared to tackle these new requirements as our governor laid out clear expectations for operating my business. My team and I were on the same page about how to safely return to work. Policing policies, reopening my salon, while rebooking three months of clients left me feeling anxious about the responsibility of providing a healthy workspace for everyone involved; it was exhausting! It was helpful that many other cities opened before us, so we were able to watch how others were handling the return. While waiting, we were able to order gloves, masks, and a variety of sanitizing products for our different surfaces. As a salon owner and leader, it was scary to be responsible for the health and safety of so many people. I realized quite quickly that it required communication, trust, and a commitment from everyone to show up healthy in our space.

So happy was I to be getting back to work, that I was completely unprepared for another peak in our civil unrest, the misinformation about COVID becoming so political, along with the waves of processing the death of George Floyd. I was unprepared for the insensitive remarks shared by some of my clients and my co-workers clients'. This issue of equality was personal for my family and the collective grief of our Black community. As a mother of biracial children and beig in an interracial marriage, I couldn't help but personalize the loss of another Black man at the hands of the police. I have family members who serve our country in the military and as police officers, and I appreciate their service. I sit in this duality, while understanding the larger system operates from bias. Polarity has been a term I use often now, and what I mean when I use it is that I often have two opposite or contradictory opinions or aspects about these realities. Multiple things are true here; racism isn't gone and the danger it can lead to is everpresent. I also know we need laws and law enforcement.

I began to see this as another opportunity to grow in my own understanding and embrace hard conversations while I was at work. I started by offering the person in my chair what I had learned about racism, offered resources, and tried to offer compassion when the ignorance on the subject reared its head. I learned that real change comes from the one-on-one moments we often share with others, this is how I continue to learn. It ultimately led to building the courage to fire a couple of clients. It was the first time in my career I had to take this stand. Surprisingly, it wasn't as hard as I thought it would be, and I experienced immense relief after I told them to leave. It was increasingly obvious to me, and those around me, that my salon and chair were a safe space for me, and that was just as important as providing safe space for others. Giving myself permission to accept that I am not for everyone was a huge lesson learned.

During the COVID times, I learned to end the glorification of being busy, and that my worth wasn't based solely on how much I accomplished. Whether it was the number of clients I served, how clean my house was, or how much I gave to others, I learned to be comfortable with slowness. I learned how to sit with my thoughts and feelings in a deeper way. I lost people I loved and couldn't go to them, or be with others to grieve during COVID. The scars and blessings I carry forward as a result of this have left me inspired by a new way of responding to people or opportunities: If it's not a "hell yes," it's a "hell no."

COVID CLIENT STORIES AND SALON LIFE

Life was challenging during the unprecedented days of the pandemic shutdown, so different than when I worked through the 9/11 attacks or the 2008 recession. Here are a few ways as a salon owner that I kept up morale and kept my business relevant and able to move forward once we reopened.

I put paper in the windows to hopefully avoid any interest in people wanting to break in or vandalize our space. It was also great for days I would go deep clean in my comfy clothes and not want to be seen. I was inspired by an idea from another local salon owner and put a "Gone Fishing" sign in the window too. I hoped to offer a smile as people passed by, it made me smile. (Thanks Amy of Adele Salon in Seattle)

I wrote regular social media posts and newsletters allowing us to offer updates and a chance to stay connected to our clients throughout our twelve-week closure. This allowed us to keep people informed, and ultimately have a smoother rebooking process for clients when it was time.

As a team we offered color kits and curbside pick up for retail products for clients. Our team would coordinate who would be at the salon to ensure only one of us was there at time. We would premix our clients' formulas for gray retouches and provide the gloves, bowls, and brushes with detailed instructions on how to do the touch up. A small thing to help us bring in some revenue, and it offered people the chance to feel more like themselves.

I had many people ask during our mandated closure if I would come to their home and cut their hair, either hinting at or saying directly, "Don't you need the money," or that they would pay extra to get a haircut or color retouch. I believe these offers were meant to be supportive, but the delivery did insult a bit, and the potential cost to my health or losing my license was not worth the risk. That being said, I was grateful to have the choice in this situation, while understanding other service providers did offer services because they couldn't go without the income.

A client started a GoFundMe for my business, and many people donated, which helped with our fixed costs: the light bill, internet, the HOA, ordering new PPE, and other small things that add up when you have no income coming in. Lots of clients offered to prepay for services or buy gift cards to support us while we were out of work. These acts of generosity carried our small business over a scary hump.

We had people express their appreciation for our commitment to the mandates and the safety of our community. We had people who complained about wearing a mask for one to two hours, while most of us double-masked for eight to twelve hours a day for almost one and a half years.

The COVID times also brought up a lot of conspiracies, and social and political tensions. Unfortunately, these did trickle into the hair appointments. We did our best to state facts, even as they changed, and stick to the science.

While a large majority understood that our policies and following the city mandates on cleanliness recommendations and capacity recommendations were for the greater good, some did not. We were challenged in the reopening to keep ourselves safe, the public safe, to be creative and inspiring while people challenged simple requests like come alone to your appointment, no pets, not to go behind the front desk and grab products, to wear their mask over their nose, to come healthy to their appointments and on time. These times required me and the team to police policies and repeat them many times, hold boundaries, and do good hair.

MY MANTRAS FOR GROWTH

Over the years, and definitely during the COVID days, I have found mantras to be a particularly useful tool to enable my personal and professional growth. Here are a few I have heard throughout my career, and how I have changed them up to work for me. I still use them today personally and in the salon when coaching.

"Do you want to be the best or the favorite?"

I heard this analogy about restaurants in a leadership workshop and it absolutely applies to service providers across the board. When you have a birthday or want to celebrate in a big way, you go to a lot of effort by getting dressed up and picking the best restaurant you can afford for that special meal because you are in search of the "best" place. That kind of outing might be once a year or less, and most people are willing to pay more than they would if it was a regular old Taco Tuesday. You also know in a year or two when you are ready to do it again there could be a new "best" place in town to try, and you are open to that. Then there is the favorite place, your favorite place might know you by name, they might know you by your food order or you by your drink order or they know you come in every Thursday after work because that is the day you work in the office. Your favorite place is reliable, where you are always met with a warm smile, and you will go to it consistently for more than just the food offerings. You spend your time telling others why they should go there, and the recommendation always includes a combination of the quality of the food and how it feels to eat there. Both are great and have a lot of benefits. I decided a long time ago I want to be better than I was yesterday and being the favorite was my goal! I wanted to do great hair, practice regularly to stay relevant, and do my best to be the warm smile and safe space that people looked forward to coming to. I wanted them to know it's okay if they aren't dressed up or are in full glam to come in. Unlike some of those fancy gyms you feel like you can't go to unless you are already in shape, I wanted it to be the place where you learn about your hair and style it. It is okay not to have it all figured out, come as you are.

"Act as if" + "Fake it until you make it."

These both ask us to be actors and play the role of someone more experienced or okay. I think this "acting" can be led by ego or even where the birth of imposter syndrome is sourced. What if you are new to the industry, why is it not okay to say that? Or maybe you're not feeling your best, physically or emotionally, I guess it wasn't okay to say that either.

My strategy now is to be honest without asking my clients to be responsible for what I am sharing. For example, if I am using a new technique or way to style, I admit to them that I am still practicing or want to practice something I learned and am excited to master it with time. If it's a physical limitation, in the consultation, I might say, I wanted to let you know my hands are having a flare-up today, so I am not able to offer a blowout, but here are a couple things we can do instead.

Some clients might catch us when we are emotionally off. If mine do and ask, I will share that I'll be okay and I have some personal things going on. Thanks for asking. Then, I move on to why we are there: the hair! I have struggled with trying to be genuine and human while still needing to "perform" in some ways; people truly count down to their appointments. Maybe it's because they just love getting their hair done and perhaps for many it's for the relationship part. Either way, it's easy to see the possibility for self-inflicted pressure to be okay or well when they ask.

I still use a version of "Acting as if" in habit building. For example, when I was starting out and building clientele, I took each client at the scheduled time to practice being on time. There were times I had hours available, but I didn't want to set a standard for clients that they didn't know how long a specific service would take. If my haircuts were an hour, I would do them in an hour. It helped build the muscle of time management and practice as if I were busy. When I would offer a pre-booking opportunity at the end, I would get them to share some times and days within my recommended return for their services rather than saying, "I have the whole day open, what works for you?" This helped to create demand and trained people not to schedule at the last minute so that way, when I was really busy, they had their preferred spot. Teaching people how to treat service providers by understanding boundaries, respecting time, and practicing clear communication is a great way to start a new client relationship. In the words of a fave, Brené Brown, "Clear is kind."

"80 percent of stylists live paycheck to paycheck, 20 percent thrive."
The first time I heard this, I was in beauty school. I heard it at countless hair shows and from seemingly every business coach that was brought in to present. I am not sure who was the first to say it, but in all these years the numbers haven't changed. Most of the industry isn't financially thriving, which means that being popular online with a big following or lots of likes doesn't equate to a stylist

being profitable. Someone's highlight reel online isn't an actual representation of how busy they are or if they are in the 20 percent living in financial security.

My take away is that consistency is the most uncelebrated, and yet most critical, part of achieving greatness. Like many industries, this one requires practicing your craft, remaining a student, and becoming a good communicator. Some of the most important education I have received has included classes on financial literacy and understanding the business of doing hair and providing services, which are critical to long-term success. These concepts apply to employees, as well as anyone who is self-employed. Your buy-in to your own success is crucial.

One way I lived the 80 percent/20 percent concept was during downtime while at work. In building or rebuilding your clientele, it is important to keep your energy up, whether you have two clients in a day or none. We enter our day at the salon with hopes someone will walk in or book online, and your mindset matters every day. The idea is to use 80 percent of your downtime related to your craft; practice a technique, research a new color trend, clean your station, create content to post on social media—this will keep your energy up and keep you well practiced. Then use the other 20 percent of your downtime to rest, go for a walk, eat, or take a brain break. Ideally, when that person walks in or someone pops up on your schedule, you are energized by the opportunity instead of feeling dread. I have seen it time and time again: When downtime is spent scrolling or gossiping in the break room, it's hard to switch into the eager, positive, and motivated creative stylist you want to be when you meet your client. When you have maintained your energy in a positive way, the one client that shows up on your open schedule can be viewed as more than income, but as an opportunity to pre-book and perhaps even gain their referrals.

"Be more interested and less interesting."

Some stylists struggle with the quiet and feel the need to perform at times, keeping the mood up and keeping clients entertained or engaged. While I do agree that the appointment should be centered on why they are there and the services you provide; we are not entertainers. I am more comfortable with silent appointments and following my client's lead on how much they want to chat once we have covered what I'm doing to their hair. While it is nice to share experiences and common interests with our clients—I'm the first to laugh and cry with someone—I do get back to why they are there, for their hair and self-care.

"It's a friendly business, and we are not friends." + "A client is more likely to become a friend than a friend is likely to become a paying client."

This is a lot to unpack, so buckle up. I have learned lots of lessons here! As a busy stylist, I've seen anywhere from eighty to over one hundred people in a month throughout my career. I often find myself thinking about people and their stories long after the appointment. I laugh, cry, and have shared some of my own personal experiences with the client, when it feels appropriate. I've been triggered by some of their stories and have had emotional reactions to what I have heard. In order to protect myself and my business, I've had to learn the art of healthy detachment. My definition of healthy detachment as a stylist is to listen with compassion while not taking on what they have shared as my own. People have shared their loss of pets, loved ones, jobs, marriages, and other sorts of traumas with me. This practice of healthy detachment is for my own well-being and enables me the ability to provide their service. As a fixer, it is hard not to be activated into problem solving mode. Understanding myself is key—I am still working at just listening as my only call to action.

I also take great pride in my work. As I often say to my clients, "Your hair and my reputation are walking advertisements for my work!" Selfishly, I'm highly motivated for each person to look their best while understanding that not everyone that sits in my chair is my friend; I have boundaries. Friendly indeed, caring, and holding space for vulnerability is guaranteed, but it doesn't mean we are meeting up for drinks.

My definition of holding space as a stylist is to provide an opportunity for people to be as vulnerable about the way they look, or want to look, and how their environment can impact the way they show up in the world.

Sometimes, clients can transition into great friends who remain clients. Sometimes, your clients will only see you as an agreeable person who takes care of them, not someone who is available to be a great exchange of energy in a healthy relationship. I have experienced both and continue to stay cautious about crossing the line with a client into the friend zone.

Some of your great friends are willing to pay full price for services with a stranger and will only see you if they get a discount, this is known as emotional discounting. I slowly cut back on my friends and family list, and now, I only offer discounts to a small handful of friends who also support my business by referring new clients to me regularly. It was no surprise to me that some of my "friends" who no longer received a discount went somewhere else to get their hair done, but most were happy to continue to support me at full price. There is no right or wrong way to handle this. Ultimately, you figure out what feels healthy for you, what allows you not to feel resentful, and what aligns with how you define professionalism. Then, you become as consistent as you can be.

"Vent sideways not downward."
Down refers to the chain of experience, not that anyone is less than, to be clear. In salon life, venting downward would look like the busy stylist, who is making great money, complaining to the front

desk worker, who is attending college part-time and working minimum wage, that their designer bag didn't arrive on time. In everyday life, it could be a parent complaining about family life or asking for advice from someone who isn't a parent and longs to be. I remember when I had my second child, and all of a sudden it was so much harder to stay organized, a friend said, "Annie, don't take advice from a parent who has less kids than you!" The same goes for any relationship, whether it's asking a single friend for advice about marriage, or, back in the salon, complaining about marriage struggles to the single, twenty-two-year-old struggling intern.

Be specific when asking for advice. Consider whether or not that person can offer a solution or guidance to your problem or if you are just dumping on them to feel better. In a work setting, there is always going to be someone who is doing less than you; they might be less busy, less experienced, or less driven than you. They might not be who you want to ask about your goal-setting habits or how to level up. Personally, being married for as long as I have, I have no idea regarding the challenges of dating or meeting people in this current world. In the same way as a parent of now adults, so much has changed from products used on babies to parenting styles, I find I can only offer encouragement, but won't offer many great solutions about raising young children in this fast-paced world. Before you ask, consider this: If they can't help you fix it, why would you share it with them? We all need a safe place to vent or share frustration, but the truth is, it does matter who you share it with.

"Be isolated so I may be elevated."

A year before leaving Arizona, I joined a very diverse women's group. It was at a church and included women of different backgrounds, ethnicities, and ages. That is where I heard a woman say she needed to be isolated before she could be elevated. For her, the context was a leap of faith to move to a new city and start fresh; it was just as true for me, too, as I was considering my move from Arizona. I have carried this with me and applied it to my personal and professional life. I don't remember her name, but I can picture her face—if she only knew how her words have stayed with me. I leaned into this message as I prepared to leave my hometown for my big move. Around this time, one of my aunts said to me, "Babe, you have outgrown your home." Some might say the universe, your angels, or it's God when the theme of the message is consistent from multiple sources. At the time, it felt like a judgmental statement my aunt made, but over time, I came to understand that what she was actually saying was that I had grown as much as I could where I was. It was time to be elevated and that required me to make some larger changes. The changes I needed to take were geographical because I had a great need to have new people around me. I had a deep understanding that the next version of me existed, and could only be unlocked, somewhere else.

"Casualness leads to casualties."

I heard this statement at a conference some years ago, and it has been a personal mantra ever since. When I heard it, I interpreted it as a very layered statement, as well as a call to action. It made me think about how we look when we show up for work. It's as simple as, are your clothes clean, is your hair done, and do you look rested? Are your tools clean and the technology up to date? Is your station clean and the last client's hair swept up? Do we speak with passion and authority about our work because we are well-practiced, or are we still learning new things? Are we continuing to be aware of perceived value in our market, as a professional, defined by us or our salon? If we are casual about our business and how we show up, we better be ready to expect clients to be casual about their commitment to us as their stylist. I am not sure about you, but I have gone to service providers I knew weren't into it, and I didn't go back. We get one chance to make a first impression.

I had a massage therapist I regularly went to, and although she liked to chat more than I preferred during a massage, she did great work. One morning it was clear something was wrong, and she shared that she suffered from migraines. I offered to reschedule or allow her to use my appointment as a break. She insisted on pushing through. Unfortunately, that meant she was suffering, and I got a less than quality massage. I was happy to extend her grace and knew this was a one off, but what if it had been my first visit with her? I'm telling you now, I wouldn't have given her another chance. My lesson here for you is: Sometimes when we push through, we aren't always hiding what's going on behind our smile as well as we think we are.

I enjoy booking a color touch-up or blow out with another salon and not letting them know I'm a stylist. Just being a regular client and paying full price for a service is a great reminder to evaluate value too. I always warn when booking that I have thick textured hair, and every now and then, I get matched with someone who I can tell that, based on their comments, isn't very into it. It doesn't feel great to be in the chair and know someone is anxious about time or doesn't prefer to work on your type of hair. I do not return to those stylists.

Maybe you only go to friends in the industry for your touch-ups or cuts. If it's within your budget, I would recommend trying to be a client in a new environment and take notes. I also make sure my friends, family, and co-workers who sit in my chair get a proper consultation—education is essential, no matter what I'm charging them. For any of us who have been around for more than ten years, staying relevant requires us to avoid complacency. We must find ways to maintain some excitement about the work. For those learning and building, consistency is so important. Don't grow casual about your goals or how you show up. And always revisit your why. It will help you keep going when the times get rough, and they will get rough.

What are some areas you get casual about when you are busy? Tired? Stressed? Don't feel well or are feeling uninspired? Evaluate and invest in yourself and your perceived value. For example, are you charging hundreds of dollars for a service and your curling iron is covered in buildup or your round brushes have bent bristles with hair in them?

I hope some of my mantras or thought provoking questions create a spark for you that you lost or possibly challenge you to look at your business with fresh eyes and even create a new "why."

What has been an unexpected rewarding benefit of your career?

"The most rewarding benefit of my career has been the different layers I've uncovered within myself. Just how much I've learned about myself through doing hair still amazes me. Hair has also brought some of the most unimaginable opportunities and people into my life. I think it has allowed me to truly exercise my true gift as well as allowed me to find a home and step into my true purpose in life, which is helping my clients see beauty within themselves, as well as see their own potential and greatness."

—ALYSSIA DOTSON, Dallas, Texas
Twenty-one years in the industry

"An unexpected benefit of my career I would have to say is the "Fake it till you become it" mentality. It has served me well. I remember starting out over thirty years ago and really being scared of everything. Scared to cut someone's hair too short, scared to mess up a color formula, scared to try and do a haircut I've never done before. But you just jump in and do it. And you learn as you go.

As I got into educating, it was the same thing. Scared to get up in front of people and speak. Nervous to walk into a salon and teach something I just learned myself. Wondering if the program I just created for a salon will be well received and inspire the stylists.

As the years went on, I realized that it's a superpower to be able to work through the anxiety and nervousness to build your skills. Don't say no. Feel the fear and do it anyway. Once you learn to accept that all new situations will create some sort of fear or anxiety, it pushes you past the fear and it becomes empowering. You start telling yourself 'I got this' instead of 'What if I can't do this.' A great life lesson."

—TAMMIE AXWORTHY, Ontario, Canada

"I was just reflecting on how valuable my early experiences were in gaining confidence through validation from clients, but over time, I have realized that the true long-term rewards come from the lessons and wisdom shared by each person, both clients & colleagues, I've worked with. The insight I've gained just by listening to their stories is like receiving free expert advice, which not only enhances my own perspective but also deepens my understanding of various industries, challenges, and personal journeys. It's a powerful way to learn and grow in my career throughout the years!"

—LORENZO SUMERA, Seattle, Washington
About forty years in the industry

"The biggest reward and benefit in my career as a hairstylist [has been] building the most intimate and vulnerable relationships with my clients. Whether I'm behind the chair, on set, or working through my nonprofit, every time I step into the role of a hairstylist, I meet incredible people. There's something so unique about getting your hair done or engaging with our industry that naturally creates a safe space. These beautiful relationships are unexpected but the most rewarding part of my work. I'm with clients during both their highest moments and some of their lowest, showing up for them and helping them feel good in a meaningful way. I honestly don't think I could've chosen a better career for that reason alone. I feel honored to be trusted, not only with how someone feels when they look in the mirror, but also with walking alongside them through their special life journey."

—ANDREA PEZZILLO, Los Angeles, California
Twenty years in the industry

"I did not expect to learn from incredible women from all walks of life in the way that I have. I was young when I entered and only really thought of trying to make a living. I feel incredibly honored to hold the stories and lessons from so many women, and it's a huge reason I decided to make this my career for the past decade."

—ALISHA NAKAMURA, Seattle, Washington
Ten years in the industry

"An unexpected rewarding benefit of my career—I've learned how connected and, in some ways, influential I am in my client's lives. Anything from day-to-day advice, hair, fashion, design, making them calm or excited (depending on the situation), and even what new tech or home goods we like. I find that I am more ingrained and, at times, personally involved in their lives than just someone who provides a service. Also, at this stage in my career, I've learned how important it is now, more than ever, to give your time and talents to help others who depend on it. But perhaps the best benefit I have found is that people in this industry will always find a way to surprise and inspire me."

—ROBERT MIDDLETON, Seattle, Washington
Thirty-six years in the industry

"I wanted to start working in the hair industry to have a fluid and creative career, something where each day was a different adventure and was always something fun and exciting. The most unexpected rewarding benefit is the people and relationships that have formed through the magic of the chair. I have always loved people, and small talk doesn't seem to be my strong suit, so it's no surprise that I quickly get to know my clients on a deeper level. What has truly touched my heart over the years is the bond that clients feel with us, their stylists, as well. How special is it that we get to walk through life during all our clients' major moments, happy or sad. We often get to be the first to learn of a pregnancy or can be a shoulder when a parent or family member has passed; we get to be a soft place to share and land through it all, and it is a role that I will never take lightly. It is such an honor to be able to be the keeper or secrets and the trusted confidant all while 'just doing hair.' That means more to me than anything, the most unexpected benefit of being a hairstylist is the soul connection with our guests, it's something that can never be taken away and truly lasts a lifetime."

—ALY MCKINNON, Long Beach, California
Eleven years in the industry

A PAGE FOR YOUR THOUGHTS

CHAPTER 4

TIME TO BUILD YOUR BOOKS

The Shag cut: A *shag cut*, also known as a wolf cut or butterfly cut, is a hairstyle that has been layered to various lengths. It was created by the barber Paul McGregor. The layers are often feathered at the top and sides. The layers make the hair full around the crown, and the hair thins to fringes around the edges.

Originating in the 1970s and experiencing a resurgence in recent times, the shag haircut showcases short-to-medium-length layers that effortlessly create a slightly messy yet chic look. It's essentially a versatile style that can work with various hair types and face shapes and a more modern version of glam rock hair.

Like this haircut you need to be flexible, a little bit fun, and a lot of business.

IS IT A CAREER OR A JOB?

We must start the conversation about building a clientele by asking ourselves if we consider this to be a career or if we believe it to be a job. A career requires you to invest time and money in education and countless hours of practice to become proficient. It requires an understanding of what the long-term commitment is; the stamina to go the distance. The outcome can be building a personal brand and legacy. The conversations you have with clients are an investment in the relationship. This investment involves understanding that what you do with their hair today impacts future options because you are thinking about their next few visits in advance. You are invested in understanding the difference between cutting layers on someone and if and why the haircut shape matters based on their face shape and lifestyle. You are paying attention to trends, knowing who to recommend them to, and when to say no. You are focused on creating an experience and considering perceived value. This mindset has to continue throughout your career, seeking inspiration and education.

A job is a short-term way to make money on your journey toward another goal. It requires some of the same concepts without as large an investment of time or commitment. You are focused on the check, just doing hair to pay the bills. In a job, you may not invest regularly in advanced education or your tools. You offer services without much thought on how they fade or grow out, not sure if you will ever see this client again. That's the next stylist's problem to fix, you think. You give the client what they want from the inspirational picture and maybe don't have an understanding on how to present better options. You are focused on just doing the hair, not nurturing the relationship with the client, and their relationship to themselves.

When you are defining your vision of success, picturing your ideal client, and outlining your financial goals, understanding if you are investing in a job or a career is crucial to the investment you will put in. The more you understand who you are and are clear about the direction you want to take, the easier it is to find your alignment in a workplace to be the kind of stylist you want to be.

When I left college to pursue a career in beauty, I knew I didn't want it to be a short-term endeavor. I was ready to find out how to get going and invest accordingly. Pursuing training and obtaining a license are the most obvious mile markers; and then, there is understanding how to build a clientele.

Here are my thoughts on building clientele: Regardless of whether you're a commission employee, renting a chair, or a stylist with your own studio, keep in mind that where you start matters. Ask yourself these questions: Is there a reputation that brings clients to the space or do you have to do the branding and start from scratch? Are you a good salesperson or do you struggle with self-promotion? No matter how you enter the industry, you will need to be able to sell yourself and know how to tell the client why they should choose you. I'll say it again: Anything that you start requires you to define what success is and who your ideal client is. Once you've decided on the type of clients you want to work with, the types of services you provide, and how busy you want to be, you can get started. Social media is a great way to market yourself, while sharing your voice and perspective. Keep in mind that stylists who have a lot of followers or likes aren't necessarily fully booked or even as financially successful as you might think. Posting to your target market is key, just like asking your clients to refer you, but be specific on what services you want to do more of by posting those pictures. On that note, not every hairstylist wants to be an influencer, and that is okay too, but understand, that in this world, having some kind of online presence is very important for your future success.

When I first started in the industry, I offered variety in my hours, from evening appointments to morning appointments and made myself available on the weekends. Offering a variety of times allowed me to capture clients with different needs. I could accommodate people coming from work, people with school-age children, and offering Saturday availability allowed me to take clients who had no flexibility during the week or only for special occasion styling. I also worked at a large salon where we had training that supported my ability to offer a wide variety of services, including haircutting, hair color, relaxers, perms, and special occasion styling. When I first got on the floor, I said yes to everything. I wanted to be good at it all. This large salon had a great reputation, and I challenged myself to retain the clients that sat in my chair. When you are the new person on the floor some clients choose you because of your price point, and some because their usual stylist is busy. An important opportunity for learning came when I realized that if you build good relationships with your front desk and make sure they understand how to support your growth, then they can book you with an ideal client! I would offer to do the support staff's and other stylists' hair so that they could personally refer me when asked about their own stylist. This also kept me busy during the slow building time; it was a chance to keep practicing my craft too. I knew building relationships was key to growth, on the team and with clients. I quickly caught on that the support staff were highly visible and often got noticed for their style. Selling myself to strangers was not easy in the beginning, so I decided I needed to create fans of my work and ask them to support me as my strategy for professional growth. So, for me, picking a salon that would provide clients based on an established brand and reputation allowed me to focus on my craft and building relationships, which allowed my clientele to grow. This environment offered so much inspiration from the creatives around me for my art. Plus, listening to how the established stylists talked to their clients and connected with them, helped me see a clear blueprint I could create for myself as a career stylist.

Once I started building a clientele and figuring out what services I preferred offering, I slowly took things I didn't like to do off my service menu. When I first started this process, I did it with my preference in mind. I didn't like doing perms anymore, so I stopped. As my career continued to grow, I niched down my service menu with my preferences, keeping my financial goals in mind. I still believe this generalized formula works for anyone who is willing to apply it. When you are starting out in this industry, it's important to try a variety of services and hours to see how you'll capture the most clients for what you enjoy doing. With that, you might be at a salon requiring you to specialize, and I would advise you to become the most well-practiced in those services. This career requires repetition, mastering techniques, formulating, communicating effectively, and building relationships.

Something to consider as you're building your clientele is whether you like long-term relationships, the challenge of knowing somebody well, and still offering fresh ideas to your clients even if you know they might not ever do it. For example, long-term relationships are slow to build and require you to stay relevant within your craft. I heard it frequently in my early days, "Offer your clients change or they will change you!" meaning that staying current on trends and helping people address hair challenges as they come up was the key to keeping my books filled with repeat clients. Just like in any relationship, the challenge is keeping things fresh. For example, sometimes I offer a cut or color change for the season or something I saw that inspired me that they have the right hair for. It is okay with me if they have no interest in a change at that time, but I want my clients to know I am thinking about them and coming up with fresh ideas for them, even if they aren't.

Another way to look at building a clientele is through short-term relationships, or what I call the "wow" factor. Everything you say is new and fresh when it comes to their hair. The short-term relationship often grows from something like a discount offer from an online or mass mailer offering a first-time discount or service specific discount, or your salon offering first-time client discounts. Oftentimes, these people deal-shop and aren't committed to any one service provider. Or, it could be the salon you're at, that they have built a reputation on walk-ins or they are located in a hotel where a percentage of the clientele is often just passing through town. These business models allow you to get a lot of first-time clients and less repeats. Your growth and future client load relies on the location visibility and the reputation of the salon.

Starting a new client relationship, even at this stage—almost thirty years into my career—is still exciting and a fun challenge, from the consultations I have with them to teaching them how to style their hair to solving their hair problems. This new relationship requires me to dig deep to see why they have sought out a new perspective. These interactions still leave me buzzing a bit. The clients that you've known for many years can still get you excited about their hair if you challenge yourself to offer them changes, or teach them how to style their hair in an updated way. This requires us to remember why they're in our chair. I've seen stylists build successful careers with either approach—either the short-term benefits of getting a full book for the week is exciting or looking out ten to twelve weeks to a full schedule. When I defined my success, my strategy was to be able to look out for weeks and see familiar clients' names on the pages. It confirmed that I was doing what I had set out to do: I was building value, relationships, and bringing in consistent paychecks.

Let's talk about a few more specific strategies in being intentional about your growth and how you fit in beauty.

ASK ABOUT SALON CULTURE

I was very naive when starting out in beauty. When I went to my first interview outside of school, I didn't know how to ask about their culture or how to even define culture in this professional salon setting. Asking about salon culture could also be interchanged for questions such as: What are the core values of this business or their guiding principles? I was clear about a couple of my professional goals, like needing more education beyond beauty school, support in attracting clients, and making a good living. I witnessed staff who appeared happy to work there; they were busy, and I knew I needed to be in a place that could help me get busy. Through my years as a stylist, what I sought out in a team or salon culture evolved as my understanding of the business progressed. Beauty school also revealed how little I knew about my chosen profession, so a salon where education and growth were provided was a no-brainer. It was through my time working that the salon culture was revealed. I figured out what my values were and that I couldn't work with people who didn't share them. Values such as cleanliness, professionalism, kindness, and surrounding myself with people who maintained their education the way I did. I learned quickly to ask those questions in future interviews. It also taught me to be clear when starting my salon to set the culture and articulate my core values clearly. I wanted those who interviewed with me to be able to make an informed decision when they considered joining my team.

SELLING YOURSELF AND KNOWING YOUR WHY ME

There is room for all of us in beauty: your style, your voice, and the way you create. I believe in showing up and sharing your passion for your craft. It's just as contagious as negative attitudes can be, so be aware of what you are spreading. People care more about the why of what you are doing than what you are actually doing. When you speak about your work, share why you started, and why you are inspired by your work. It's important to understand who you are and why you want to be in the industry. It's easier to get people excited about why they should sit in your chair, why they should rebook a follow-up appointment or why they should refer you to their friends and family. For example, when first meeting someone at a party or at your partner's work function, a common question as people are making introductions is, "What do you do for a living?" I do hair, doesn't sound that exciting or inspiring and is rarely met with a follow-up question. You might get a response of "Cool" or an anecdote of how much they love their hairstylist. Maybe you could answer, "I help people define their personal style and express their identity through their hair, the one thing they can't take off." Find your why, and when people ask you the "What do you do" question, tell them your why. This opens up more curiosity about your craft and perhaps brings them to seeing you as a passionate professional. Consider even how you post on socials: Is your why coming through? Are you sharing what you love about your clients, your love of the process of doing hair and why you keep going?

THE CONSULTATION

To me, the best ones are seen as a collaboration of our client's ideas and our experience articulated professionally.

I think of a consultation, the start of every appointment, as setting out for an epic road trip. You need some basics before heading out, but mainly, you need to know where you are going, and what it takes to get there from everyone who wants to join the fun. I have followed the script below as my road map and adapted it throughout the years based on whether the client is new to me or is established. This form of communication takes practice and a plan. It is important to gather all the information and have enough time for the services. When you rush or don't stick to your plan, it increases the chance for redoes and keeps you from building trust for the long-term relationship. This formula I follow isn't an original idea, I took it from Framesi, the brand I taught for previously, and customized it throughout the years to fit my style. Once practiced, I coach and stick to consultations that should not be more than fifteen to twenty minutes, if it's running a lot longer, that is a signal you might not be a good fit for this particular client.

Listen. This step is about gathering information by asking a couple specific questions to get them talking about their hair history and goals. What do they currently like or don't like about their hair as it is today? Even with a trained eye, you can't go back in time eight weeks or six months to when they loved it. While pictures are a great tool, I like to get them talking first. I also will make sure to get them talking about their lifestyle, how often they wash, the different ways they style their hair and the tools they feel comfortable working with when styling. This is also the time to listen for problems and is a great opportunity to recommend services, products, or tools to address them as well. Keep in mind, sometimes they have all the right products or tools and no one has ever shown them how to use them and when.

Share. This is when I share my professional recommendations based on their goals and hair history. I focus on one part of the service at a time, like the haircut, and confirm why I agree with the inspiration pictures and refer back to their lifestyle and the maintenance of this style. Other times, I consider this an opportunity to share some modifications I would make to their idea in order for it to best work for their life, texture, and maintenance goals. Then, I switch to the hair color; it's a similar process, the how and why this would look good with their skin tone, how often they would need to refresh the look or maybe why I think a few modifications could be a better fit to maintain the integrity and fabric of their hair. I make sure they know the frequency needed to maintain this look and the total cost.

Clarify. This is the time to consolidate ideas and get clear on the direction: their inspiration plus the reality of the look from a cost, styling effort, and up-keep perspective. It could sound like, "To get this light with your dark hair, we will need two or more sessions and that is going to cost about four hundred dollars." Or I might say, "To get this haircut shape you desire we will need to grow out this part of your hair while shortening your length." It's at this time that I will often share a style change if they are new or not, their hair already has an existing story, there is a shape in their hair that can contribute to or limit our options. Your hair color history or current haircut impacts your future options. It is very rare these days that someone comes in with virgin hair, an industry term for no artificial hair color or highlights. It is 100 percent their natural color. So the existing story determines the type of color or highlight history in their hair, and the coloring over previous highlights to match the natural color means the hair has still had that process—it doesn't disappear because it was covered up. In the same way it is rare to have someone come in with long unlayered hair looking for a new shape, most are coming in with a haircut shape that limits the possibilities for big change. I love the following analogy: For people who have previous color or are looking to change up an existing haircut shape, imagine your hair is like the coloring book at the doctor's office that has been colored in. I am going in and contributing to the existing art, but it's not all my work or a complete vision after one visit. I let people know that if we decide to move in a new direction, it can take anywhere from two to four sessions to get to a goal. Managing expectations through these conversions is key. It's great if you can underpromise and overdeliver.

Ask Permission. This step is often skipped over and can lead to redoes or negative reviews very quickly. Before you wash or run away to mix color, it's a quick question to ask: "Do you have any final questions as we have covered so much? Do you feel good about our plan and can I get started?" You would be surprised how many people will chime in with a couple more questions or concerns, and this final step of consent does help ensure that we are both mutually taking responsibility in the commitment.

Take Action. This sounds so easy. I have heard stories from clients who came to me for correction work about how confused they were that a disaster like this happened. Many times I would hear recounts from them that the consultation went great, but then the stylist would just go do whatever they wanted, and the end result was a very unsatisfied client who vowed never to go back to that salon and get their hair done again. This step is a reminder to stick to the plan, stay on task, and do not change the course you have committed to, before or during the service, unless you and your client are in agreement.

Sometimes, even after following a well-planned-out consultation formula like the above, it can become clear that the consultation wasn't as thorough or clear as you thought it was. This results in the client asking questions, perhaps while you are applying the color. These questions often look like:

- "So are we doing highlights?"
- "Will all my gray hair be covered?"
- "How often do I have to get this touched up?"
- "How long will this take?"

These kinds of questions are definite signs that you need to start the consultation over or go back to the missed steps and get their permission to continue.

An unclear consultation can also result in the client asking questions that clarify the direction during the haircut, such as:

- "Will it still reach into a ponytail?"
- "Can I still wear it straight and curly?"
- "How often will I have to come in to keep this new shape?"

These are your clues to tighten up your consultations and have clearer communication. Cost, maintenance, and how they wear their hair should be a part of the consideration right from the start and revisited as they are leaving. It's common to get questions during the service or at the end, ideally these questions lean toward styling and how this new hair could impact future changes, that is a good sign your consultation was thorough.

CONSULTATION STORIES

Here are some examples of how I've approached consultations:

Scenario: A client brings in a reference photo of a woman with hair blowing in the wind. The model is wearing a hat as her color inspiration.

Example: It wasn't quite clear to me what the client was asking for, so I began by asking her some questions after we had a giggle. What does she see specifically that she likes? I share what I see. It ended up that there was a highlighted strand and she loved the color of the blonde in it; she wanted her pieces to have that tone. Our clients don't know all the technical terms, and photos are often the best way to communicate what they don't have the words for—it's our job to translate their vision to the desired outcome.

Point: Even the most outrageous photos a client brings in can be inspiration.

*   *   *

Scenario: Texture conversations. I have had, on more than one occasion, people bring in photos of hair that is a completely different texture and want to know if they can have it.

Example: A girl with long, straight, thick hair asks what treatments could give them the outcome of fine, curly hair. Or the other side, someone with fine, thin hair bringing in a picture of a person from a different race with curly hair asking how to achieve that look. This is where I often lead with a joke, "This sounds like

a conversation to have with your parents, and we can't change our genetics."
On a more serious note, we talk through the pros and cons of perms and other
chemical services that are available.

Point: Don't assume what is so obvious to you is known to others. For example,
something I still educate people on is that your hair grows from your scalp not
your ends. My goal is to provide my professional opinion from my experience to
help them make an informed decision.

*   *   *

Example: I've had a new client calling in and they are frustrated because they've
tried many salons and no one ever gets it right. When trying to match her with
a stylist, it was clear she had no idea what she wanted. I shared with her that
without a clear vision or reference photo, it wasn't possible for me to refer her to
a stylist, let alone add her to the schedule without an idea of the type of service
she wanted. I recommended a complimentary consultation and for her to do
some research before she came in.

Point: I educate clients that if their relationship is ever going to be successful with
any stylists, they have to show up prepared. It helps us as stylists to know things
they like or don't like, we are not mind readers nor do we have magic wands. It
takes their realistic understanding of their hair plus our artistry. Coming in with
no clear direction is like going on a road trip without charting a course or having
a destination in mind, which is why managing expectations—and explaining the
hows and whys—is so important in a consultation.

*   *   *

Scenario: A client sits down in the chair and says they would like something
different . . . but they aren't willing to do anything different.

Example: Consultations in this scenario often have statements like:

- "I want something totally different, but I don't want to lose any length, and I don't like to style my hair."

- "You know I don't like to style my hair, and here's a photo of a new style I am considering." Then they hand over a photo of highly-styled hair.

- "I really want movement and volume, but I want my hair long with no layers."

- "I hate my frizzy hair, but I don't want to use heat to style, and I don't like products."

- "I loved my hair for about two months after you first did it, and I hate it now. I only want to come in twice a year. Can you fix it?

- "Twenty years ago, my hair used to look like this." Then they show a photo, referring to thickness or the color. "Can you recreate it?"

Point: These consults can get us lost. I've found that managing expectations while bringing the conversation to what they currently like or do not like about their existing hair has helped me stay on task. I acknowledge them by saying something like, "I hear you are bored while not ready to maybe take a big leap." I offer a small tweak to a haircut option, like a little texture in the perimeter or some long facial framing. If it's a color we are doing, sometimes as small as a slight tone change. If these feel too big, I offer no change and teach them a new way to style, a fresh idea on a bun, pony, or how to use an iron to reinvent. This allows them to get some change, and know that I am listening without judgment about not being ready.

TAKEAWAYS

One question I commonly receive from clients when they are considering a change is, "Do you think it will look good on me?" I am very direct during my consultations about flattering looks for a client's hair texture and face shape, often using clothes as a reference to visualize. A good haircut is like finding a cut of jeans that flatters your figure, we can all relate to a great pair of jeans that makes us feel confident. I also share my second motivation, which can be perceived as selfish; if they look good, I look good. A happy client with a flattering hairstyle is the best kind of business card. I am highly motivated for people to leave my chair feeling confident, equipped with the ability to recreate the look at home, in between visits to me, since they are a walking advertisement of my work. Sure, there are times clients decide to go against my recommendation. Sometimes people really want to try a tone of color or length I think might not be the best fit, and I give them all the information I can to make an informed decision. But at the end of the day, it's their decision.

I often use a quote I heard from a mentor of mine about twenty years ago: "It's their hair and my reputation." So I do refuse services if I believe their hair can't handle the transformation or recommended doing it over the course of several sessions to maintain the health of their hair. In my experience, the times I went against my gut and knew they weren't ready for the change or their hair couldn't get to the color they desired and I still went for it, it led to redoes, a lot of support calls on how to style and grow, and just a whole lot of stress (Thank you Jo Blackwell-Preston, A.W.E Salon, NYC).

One of my biggest takeaways is that, when you invest in the client relationship, it has an unexpected side effect of building trust, committing to solving problems together, and partnering through hard times. For me, it has resulted in twenty-one years in Seattle, retaining many clients from day one who have traveled many locations with me and paid my price increases.

Some have stayed in my salon as a continued support of my business and no longer see me for a variety of reasons like my price, our schedules no longer working, or wanting a new set of eyes on their hair. I made sure they were comfortable enough to ask for the referral or to stay in the space without feeling uncomfortable. I've had clients not follow me for a variety of reasons throughout the years too and reach out to rebook or ask for referrals within my team. I have a deep appreciation for this trust and their understanding they are always welcome back. I want what's best for every single person who sits in my chair, even if it's only once!

How do you feel after your hair appointment, ie; pretty, confident, uplifted?

"I always feel restored and refreshed after I see Annie. While I leave feeling pretty (and even younger), it's much more than that. I have such gratitude to Annie for including me in her life, sharing our ups and downs, and deeper goals of our personal growth. We are two women offering complete attention with each other, responding with curiosity, empathy, laughter, and sometimes even tears. In the many years of being her client, I feel appreciated, understood, and loved. What more can you ask of your hairstylist?"

—GEORGI S.
Seattle, Washington

"The short answer to how I feel after leaving a hair appointment is lighter, confident, educated, supported, and grateful. After leaving a hair appointment the overwhelming feeling of 'light' offers double meaning. Not only do I experience the physical feeling of light with less hair, whether a trim or a style change, there is also the emotional feeling of light that overcomes me as I leave my appointment. The bond with my stylist and the physical space in which they fill is an important part of the experience of my hair appointment. My time in the chair is much needed and valued hairapy.

Having a stylist that offers me a safe space to speak to, laugh with, and learn from is an absolute treasure! The comfort to try something new paired with the confidence for my look as I receive education and tips on how to blow out a bob or which way to curl long layers is invaluable. In my opinion, it takes a very special person to be a stylist. Someone who has chosen an industry in which they service all walks of life and live through countless clients' ups and downs yet offer their full attention and support to the person in their chair in the present moment is without a doubt a superpower. I am beyond grateful for the gift of my stylist."

—TRISH S.
Phoenix, Arizona

"I feel confident and radiant after my hair appointments; I seem to walk away with an extra pep in my step. I also feel seen as a woman, mother, wife, and professional, and appreciate our conversations."

—SARAH S.
Seattle, Washington

A PAGE FOR YOUR THOUGHTS

CHAPTER 5

MAKING MOVES

The Mullet Cut: The *mullet cut*, aka business in the front and party in the back, is characterized by shorter hair in the front and on the sides, with the hair longer in the back. This classic style, often associated with the '70s and '80s, is making a comeback in modern trends. The key features of a mullet are the contrast between the shorter, often tapered or faded sides and front, and the longer, more flowing hair in the back.

Almost fifty years after it became famous, mullet hair is back, softened, with more layers and less contrast with the long back. It is gender-neutral and is modified depending on the texture of your hair. This cut is more versatile than ever, and it can be styled differently from day to night to embrace how multifaceted we are.

THE MANY OPTIONS FOR MOVEMENT

Let's talk about all the ways you can move in the biz as a hairstylist. You can change locations and still work for the same company. For example, the salon I started working at had multiple locations in one city. As an apprentice, you would rotate salons initially, having the opportunity to learn from different educators. Once you finished the haircutting portion, you could start on the floor one day a week, taking clients. My single day got busy with updos and haircuts. Once my color and chemical education was complete, I could transition to a full-time stylist. The location was chosen by the leadership based on where they thought I would grow and that also had an open chair.

I have seen some people, shortly after completing their education, go out on their own or move salons. This can be tricky, depending on how established you are and the salon's policy on your client list; a move like this can feel like starting over all together. Social media has made this a little easier for stylists to stay connected with their clients for a smoother transition, but it's still hard. I have had to navigate this as a stylist and a salon owner.

As a stylist moving around within the same city, I started to keep a record of my clients so when I moved I could inform them where I was going. I maintained my pre-booking even if I knew a move was coming and then would contact them to let them know, same day and time but to please come to the new location. Most people already allot time for travel so the new location, which was often not too far away, wasn't an issue. If it was, I would offer a reschedule based on the new location and their commute. And how far I moved impacted the number of clients who followed me. The old adage is that if you move any further than two miles away from your current salon, expect to lose 60 percent of your business. Unfortunately, I have found this to be pretty accurate.

The biggest move, obviously, comes with changing cities or states. It continues to be celebrated in this industry that our careers are flexible, and, I guess from the outside it can appear that way. Yes, we can start over with our skill set anywhere, anytime. The misconception is that you can immediately replace your income. That simply isn't true. Every time you move, it's important to consider the percentage of clients that are willing to follow you and the opportunity present at the new place, and weigh the two. Starting over in a new city definitely took me back to my early days and reactivated all the lessons I had learned about building a clientele. The importance of consistency in availability, communication about changes to my business, and a great consultation and service helped me get grounded in rebuilding.

WHY STYLISTS LEAVE SALONS

It can be as simple as a long commute or that you prefer the products used at a different salon. Many stylists leave because of a toxic work environment or finding out that the salon culture isn't what they had signed up for or revealed itself to be over time. Things that I have personally seen at my work places and would consider toxic include sexual harassment, affairs with clients or within the team, leadership bullying—personal attacks that had nothing to do with their work, and an employee having a verbal blow up that led to throwing items at me and other employees. Some of these could fall under culture too, as in the leadership didn't offer a defined code of conduct when issues did arise, therefore we could not trust that issues would be handled. The lack of defined culture or understanding of expectations led me to leaving salons because the toxic behaviors made for an unsafe space for me mentally and physically.

I stayed for several years at the salon where I completed my apprenticeship. I knew this place was special, from the education opportunities that allowed me to grow as well as the opportunity to travel. With all that said, I knew deep down that I no longer fit in the town after a while, and if I didn't leave soon, I never would. I was breaking up with the town where I had experienced many personal tragedies and professional wins. I started to invest in healing myself and my relationships through exploring more spiritual practices and counseling before I left. I wanted to know I had given it all I could before leaving. My children were at a stage where starting over had the potential to go smoothly. Ideally, I wanted to get them settled before they left elementary school. After seven years of a successful salon career in my hometown, I moved to Seattle in December 2004. I picked Seattle because it offered a nonstop flight for my children to visit family. I liked that it was still on the West Coast, and I really liked the weather. It had built in seasons for rest; growing up in a place where it was sunny all the time had left me with a mentality of survival rather than thriving. I joke that I left the desert because I needed to be watered, mentally and spiritually. So I picked a place where things were growing all around and believed that could be contagious. I knew starting over would be hard, and that I would need the grit that it would require to build a new clientele, which added to the pressure I felt to provide for my family as a single mom. Even knowing all of this, I sold my house and downsized my personal belongings. I knew it was time to take the leap. It was hard to say goodbye to everyone, and as a result, I sat in that grief while I anxiously anticipated my next chapter with my kids.

When I started to look for salons in Seattle, my naivety revealed itself once again. I had lived and worked in one place, and because of that, I expected to move and find a replacement salon without realizing that a salon or the feeling I had at my old salon might not exist in my new city. I always had an appreciation for where I had started my career. Leaving revealed how special of a place it truly was. My first salon was not perfect, it was filled with humans, afterall, but it did have a defined culture and leadership that offered accountability and support. So in the messiness of creative people finding their way, it provided a sense of safety in the workplace for me. And I realized that was difficult to replicate.

I quickly learned that no matter how impressive my resume was or what I had previously contributed in my industry, I really was starting over. I researched several commission-salon opportunities within twenty miles of where I lived. I decided to make this bold move because I wanted to work in the city, not the suburbs. That shortened the list of salons I was interested in working for. So, I got dressed up, made sure my portfolio represented my best work, printed out copies of my buttoned-up resume, and started the interview process. I was so optimistic when I started out, my irrational confidence was at a ten! My last salon had created a reputation that preceded our small town, as did my reputation as an educator and successful stylist. It was a no-brainer that I was a great hire. I quickly learned that while those things got me in the door for the interview, what ultimately would get me hired was the answer to the question, *Do you have any clients to bring with you?* No, was the answer that ended almost all the interviews, to which they inevitably responded, "Thanks for coming, and if you get some clients, feel free to reach back out." I had gotten better at this point at selling myself, and I assured them that any client that sat in my chair as a result of the reputation of their salon, would stay because I would be able to keep them and grow the relationship. This was not enough to get me hired at any of my top picks. It was clear that once I got enough clients, I could reach back out. I considered myself to be a loyal person, so the tension of thinking about this option of getting clients and changing salons was new, and it was a light-bulb moment to realize that the most important person to be loyal to was myself. I deserved my peace and my success. This meant adjusting my mindset and working at a place to start building a clientele without the pressure of it being my forever salon.

After moving to Seattle, I worked in four commission salons. At first, these stats felt like a failure, but now, I see it as growth. I'm proud now to say, the first salon I worked in I quit after only two weeks. It was chaotic and I knew it was not the place for me, so I moved on. The next salon I worked at only lasted for six weeks because I recognized that they didn't align with my values. I had never been talked down to or witnessed others being talked down to in such a nonprofessional way like I experienced there. I challenged myself daily to "Get thicker skin, Annie!" And then I realized my skin was just fine and even got so bold as to say to the owner, "Don't mistake my professionalism and respect for honoring how you want your clients taken care of as ignorance. I am talented." I witnessed a long list of things there that left me unsettled so after six weeks, I quit. That was all I had to give. I also took away from this experience something very valuable: Just because it was a cool, fancy salon in a big city, full of talented artists, there was no excuse for so much toxic behavior, and might I say abuse, to be normalized. This pride I felt for leaving quickly came from my personal growth; I was gaining the ability to recognize unhealthy people or places and giving myself permission to remove myself from them without taking on the responsibility of needing to fix it. Even more astounding was that I was realizing how unwilling I was to change myself, morph if you will, in order to fit in. This was real growth. That was a huge win for me as I focused on creating my new life.

I landed my third salon position at a start-up, which made me super nervous, but the owner knew of my salon in Tucson, so that felt great; she got me! This salon had some cool new ideas, like incorporating a med spa, a wardrobe stylist, and on-site makeup. Clients loved this one-stop shop. I was able to build up a good client list and made some lifelong friends there. Unfortunately, once again, the unhealthy parts of this environment made it clear that another move was inevitable. I lasted a year and reached back out to a previous salon who had turned me down until I had a client base to bring with me. I was hired at my fourth salon, and thankfully, it was a soft landing. The owner was kind, honest, and had a lot of experience in running her business. She explained to me that growing beyond the clients I had brought with me would be my responsibility. This salon had a great reputation and was committed to feeding new clients to recent graduates from their apprenticeship program, which meant new referrals for me would be limited. This is a common practice and definitely something to consider if you change salons or cities and hope to grow your clientele. This place offered a couple of personalities that kept me on edge but the leadership, education, and professionalism felt so great! Overall, it was a refreshing experience. Yet, after a year of working there, I was still not experiencing a lot of growth. That, combined with the cost of working downtown, started to add up, and my savings were nearly gone. I knew if Seattle was going to be home, I had to get things clicking quickly—it was time to make another leap of faith. Giving my notice to the owner who offered me refuge was very emotional, I was nervous she would think I took the opportunity she had given me for granted. I cried my way through the conversation and she was incredibly supportive.

My next opportunity came when a former co-worker who I trusted and respected said the salon she was at was regularly turning away clients. After talking with the owner it seemed like a good move, the location allowed for a shorter commute and there was free parking, which was a big money saver. I started at my first lease salon and things really took off. This salon was small and the team was very kind as they supported me in making this transition. I stayed for five years at that location and learned so much more about the business side of hair. I quickly learned I loved using that side of my brain. This opportunity allowed me to work as hard as I wanted, have flexible hours, and use the products I loved.

I'm grateful for all the salon owners who took a chance on me. I'm grateful for the community I made within the industry along the way. And I am also grateful that I learned what an unhealthy work environment looks like, making it easier for me to recognize them, and the healthy ones, moving forward. I felt empowered, encouraged, and committed to finding my place to make this move work for my family.

Salon life was so different in my new city in so many ways. Salon professionals dressed more casually; previously, there was an all-black dress code and no jeans. Now, I had to figure out my personal style in my new city without hiding behind the all-black clothes. Hairstyles and products were different too—they had to be weather-friendly, as the humidity and misty rain were pretty constant, instead of dry-climate friendly, which requires different care. The conversations were different too. There was a casual tone and less rigidity to the salon culture. The frequency of returning clients was much longer than what I was used to. In Arizona, clients returned anywhere from four to eight weeks. In Seattle, clients were returning mostly in the eight-to-fourteen-week range and even semi-annually. I quickly learned that to replace my income, I would need to, at minimum, double my previous clientele.

When I was getting ready to leave Tucson, I will never forget the conversation I had with my boss Pam, the owner of the company. I explained my reasons for wanting to move to Seattle, and she quietly listened, nodding every once in a while, but then she said something that was so profoundly true and valid, and I think of it often. "You are a survivor, and your instinct is to survive. Make sure that before you leave, you figure out if you're starting over to make things hard again so you can survive, because thriving feels so uncomfortable." I blinked hard and tried to process what she was saying. Yikes, she had seen right through me! I had yet to make that connection in my healing journey. When one has experienced trauma and independence as young as I had, it's normal to become comfortable with uncomfortable situations. She wasn't wrong. For the first time, I was thriving and not in survival mode. It didn't change that I knew that my next level of growth couldn't happen in the same place as the pain. I also knew deep down I wasn't running from anything; I had faced the demons of my past the best I could at that time, and I was ready to take the leap. I still check in on this when I am considering a big leap or change. All these years later I still can't believe that with hundreds of employees, Pam saw me, spoke truth into me, told me I would be welcomed back and sent me off with well wishes.

Before I left, another trusted leader at my company, Frank, asked me, "Something to think about before you leave: This might not be the town you love, but you're building a great career. What if your success just allows you to travel more without moving?" Ultimately, I decided not to try; I had decided that leaving on good terms gave me peace. If Seattle wasn't my place, I could return to my wonderful job and hopefully regain some of my amazing clients. The example he gave was the ability to be a big fish in a little pond versus leaving and becoming a small fish in a big pond. This actually excited me; all I could think of was new waters to explore and a fresh start. I needed to find my place where I could be my whole self.

The hard truth is that it took me over two years to pay my bills without relying on savings. I provided discounted haircuts out of my house to new mom friends who wouldn't go to the city or who helped me out with my kiddos. I had new friends offer haircut days for cash at their house to introduce me to their friends for potential clients. By year two and a half, my savings were gone. I stayed the course, asking clients to send me their friends, trying to create diversity in my clientele and services to offset how infrequent some would come in. It was year three when things really started to click in my new world. My books had filled in more, I had created demand and established relationships that led to clients pre-booking with me, and now had consistent income. I stayed the course, even when it didn't look promising.

I prefer to use the word choice versus sacrifice, though sometimes they can be interchangeable. On occasion, the choices I made limited other choices, and this phrasing allows me to feel less resentment when the hard part kicks in. I have to acknowledge that it is a privilege to be in a position to have choices. I did make some choices "sacrifices" throughout the journey and it wasn't always easy. For example, my kids and I didn't have community in the same way, we didn't vacation for a few years other than exploring our new area because of finances. I put on pause some of the other creative outlets for a bit and didn't travel far for teaching, I had to keep in mind the distance away from my kids since without a lot of support it no longer made sense to travel far. I needed to put all my efforts into being behind the chair to build my clientele and being available to my kiddos as they acclimated into their new worlds. While at times I got lonely and felt scared about the choice to be so far from all my familiar things, I had a deep understanding and belief that it would be okay. I no longer had a group of friends to have a couch hang or happy hour with and with the salon moving I did, it was slow to make work friends too. I did enjoy the gift of anonymity at times and the chance to reinvent myself even with the discomforts. The gift of starting over is that you enter the spaces new. I could start new friendships based on the direction I was going, not just because we had shared history. In my experience, some of my old relationships had a hard time accepting my changes, my new way of seeing things or being. They weren't on the same speed of change and they preferred the old me. I learned it was okay to be picky about who I let into my life, and was blessed by a couple of deep connections early on in this new adventure. It was a smaller circle, but it was created with intention. Regarding dating, I felt strongly that if my dates were going to take energy away from my very full life, then it was a no for me. They had to be an attribute, aligned, not a drain. I met the person who became my husband in 2007 and am currently in my twentieth year in Seattle. We are celebrating our sixteenth year of marriage this year, 2025. My kids consider the Pacific Northwest home, so yes, it was absolutely worth the choice to start over and make the choices, though some would say sacrifices, that came along with it.

I can now reflect with pride on how much growth this change brought me. The chance to experience other ways of living and a new-found appreciation of seasons and nature have allowed me to grow too. I have learned that even when things seem hopeless, once you grieve, it can be an opportunity to change directions. I am not always positive or hopeful, but I do get myself back on track through reflecting on all the things I have already overcome, self-inflicted or not.

A REFLECTION FOR YOU

What is a choice you are scared to make because it changes other potential choices? Are you willing to sacrifice for a period of time to get to the outcome or content just talking about the possibility? What drives you to work hard, travel, have financial security and independence, have a savings account of a certain amount, or maybe all of these things and more? Do the choices you make daily align with those desires, like wanting to be healthy; do your daily choices like food choices, water intake, and movement support that desired outcome the majority of the time? Creating your ideal professional life or income requires the same disciplines, and a way to measure the metrics of successful actions.

A PAGE FOR YOUR THOUGHTS

CHAPTER 6

THE RELATIONSHIPS

The Curly Cut: A *curl-defining haircut* is a specialized technique designed to enhance and shape curly hair, resulting in more defined and bouncy curls. It typically involves cutting the hair dry, curl-by-curl, to preserve the natural curl pattern and minimize frizz.

Ideally, individual curls are cut to maintain their shape and prevent bulk or unevenness. Layers are strategically added to remove bulk and create movement, while avoiding the removal of weight from the ends, which is crucial for defining the curl. These haircuts are tailored to individual curl types, face shapes, and desired styles.

Like curls and a curly cut, relationships can be a bit bouncy and change with the weather.

BEING IN THE CHAIR IS A GOOD TIME TO SHARE

As a stylist and human who appreciates deep connections and building long-term relationships, I am still surprised by the unbelievable things people have entrusted me with, and I am referring to things way beyond their hair. People share their highest highs with me, like engagement announcements, pregnancy news, the fact that they found their birth family, or got the position they were striving for. They will tell me their stocks cashed in for an obscene amount of money, a surprise inheritance amount was left to them and the opportunity to buy their dream house or retire early. I have also witnessed horrible lows, like deaths in the family, illnesses that change lives irreversibly, marriages ending and the reasons for that end, as well as horrible stories of abuse or the devastating loss of a job they just couldn't afford to lose.

It was clear I was unprepared to hear their stories, and I needed to learn how to manage my expressive face and reactions to these highs and lows. It started with learning to manage my personal judgments and being open to other experiences beyond my understanding in order to create a safe space for whoever was sitting in my chair. I watched mentors of mine navigate this and asked for help on how to politely shift conversations back to hair, the reason we were there, so we could keep the appointment moving forward. Remaining in a space that is judgment free is a process I continue to work on. The kind of depth I experience in having long-term relationships is beautiful, fulfilling, and requires effort, professionally and personally. My love of these connections is a blessing, and a burden, at times. I am still learning that holding space for others doesn't require me to fix anything or take on their burden as my own. It just asks that I listen and let them know I care. I know many industry friends who feel strongly about maintaining clear boundaries around deep sharing with their clients. Sometimes, I wish I was wired that way. I often think about how much lighter I would probably feel at the end of the day if I didn't allow those deeper conversations to take place between me and my client as I am painting highlights and folding foils. After many years of practice, I accept that this is who I am, and my responsibility has been to learn healthy boundaries through detachment with the goal of avoiding my own emotional overwhelm. Not everything everyone shares with me is for me to fix or carry—I am still working on this mantra and practice.

The other part of my responsibility to the client who is sharing with me is to be a resource, but to avoid overstepping in the advice arena. I have done this too many times to count. I have overshared personal stories in trying to connect to theirs, or I have offered advice when it wasn't asked for and I have received big emotional reactions because I had things going on beyond what they were sharing. I am aware of the trust people put in me and to take care when sharing recommendations, whether it's a book or a therapist I have trusted. As is with everything else, I'm still learning the art of this too. A mantra I practice is, "I am an expert of my story and experiences only." If I offer advice, I try to phrase it like, "In my experience, this was helpful." There is no perfect formula for this, or a right way to connect; it just comes down to being authentically you and learning from when you miss the mark.

HAIRAPY

While we are in no way qualified for the role, oftentimes when a client sits down in the chair, we immediately become a "hairapist" for them. Here are some experiences I have attempted to artfully navigate as a stylist.

I might ask you where you part your hair two to four times during your appointment but I never forget how you felt when you shared . . .

Weddings

About five years ago I was working a wedding in which the sister of the bride just could not let the day be about the bride. She kept talking over her, laughing at the way her makeup turned out, and texting when she should have been attending to her sister. I kept it professional and didn't say anything even though I've watched friends, sisters, and mothers of the bride who couldn't help but make the day about them, whether it was about how they looked or needing more attention. This happened at both of my weddings too, these big days can be really uncomfortable for people who love you and don't know how to express it, so sometimes they act out a bit or maybe feel left out because it's not about them, so they create a scene of some sort.

I've had more than one bride confide in me that they were already married, but no one knew. Some decided to do it to take the pressure off the day, some shared that they did it for financial and tax reasons, or some just wanted their moment to be protected and the chance to share vows they didn't feel comfortable saying in front of their families or communities.

I have witnessed interracial relationships of all combinations who either had to leave family out of their weddings because of racism, the lack of support of the union, or had opted not to have a big wedding because they couldn't bring everyone together. I, too, know this tension of not trusting if you can have everyone together and how it would go in order to have a safe space.

On a similar theme, same-sex couples sometimes need to make the same decisions about leaving family out, to include their parents or not, or they simply don't have a large wedding because of the lack of support from family. Even when you know your partner is the right choice for you, I remember the grief shared when people are not supporting you and your love. Some are led to relief that they don't have to be uncomfortable as they celebrate their love.

I have overheard some of the kindest words of encouragement and support shared between friends, sisters, and parents to the bride. I have seen thoughtful gifts or beautiful letters delivered to brides on their big day from their new spouse, parents, or new bonus kids. I have witnessed countless tears shed as brides prepare for their day after losing a parent or a loved one. Losing my dad young, I tend to be the crying stylists in the corner when the dad comes in to see his daughter for the first time or when he walks her down the aisle, I just can't help it.

I have been well fed, given beautiful gifts as a thank you, and invited to stay at many weddings.

When doing weddings, you can be asked to set up in a hotel room, hotel conference room, someone's personal bathroom, even shoved in a closet, to get the bridal party ready. As a stylist you just make it work and you learn to bring more than your hair tools. I started traveling with extension cords, fans, chairs, cleaners, paper towels, and countless other things.

Non-hair-related things I have assisted with on the big day range from making sure the bride has something to eat or drink while getting ready to playing security, the bride telling me before the day who she needed to keep away from her while she got ready. I have helped direct other vendors to their locations. There were times I was asked to help advise on décor or how to capture and style a picture. I have helped to repair shoes, undergarments, and dresses. I've assisted when a bride or mother of the bride has had a panic attack and helped the best I could to help them create space from others, fan them, cool down the room, or get water. There have been plenty of hungover people who needed a little assistance in getting it together without alarming the bride. I stayed to help when the wedding was called off the day of, notifying guests and vendors it wasn't happening.

Life events

At the first salon I worked at, we were near a major university that often had color corrections from sorority girls who got drunk and decided to dye each other's hair. The line we shared with them was that the seven-dollar box cost them or their parents a few hundred. This was always funny to me—a few drinks down, and someone in a group says, "I can do your hair!"

I love birth stories; I invite any new mom who sits in my chair to share as much as they feel comfortable. I have heard tragic stories about stillborn babies, things going unplanned and scary during delivery, surprises about the gender they were told they were having, partners not making it in time, beautiful adoption stories from long travels around the world including being invited into the delivery room, and adoption stories that result in long battles. A favorite of mine is from one long-term client—probably because I truly enjoy her, and she's a great storyteller. It was her first baby, and my first time seeing her after delivery. She began by saying, "I am starting at the end. I had the baby in our Suburban, in the parking lot of the hospital. We will keep this car and make our daughter drive it when she's of age." We laughed so hard as she filled in the rest of the story.

I have received calls from women or their partner on the way to the hospital because they went into labor early or emergency surgery and wouldn't make their upcoming hair appointment. I am shocked every time this happens, and it reminds me how beautiful our connection is. In turn, this kind consideration is juxtaposed against people who had a cold or flu and did not call to cancel, then don't respond to my message, only to call weeks later asking to get back in, and then get frustrated when I can't accommodate them quickly. I give grace in those situations, and for some, it became a pattern that when illness or life got big they wouldn't show up or cancel, so I ultimately had to have the conversation that I could no longer be their hairstylist. I was met with frustration, defensiveness, and they were often offended. Sitting in that tension with them isn't easy but holding my boundary so I could count on my income or how my day would flow in the future was always worth it.

I have had the honor to provide many first haircuts and meet these little people I have witnessed come to be over the course of years sometimes. Yes, there are often tears on my end.

I've had clients' partners join the consultation and have strong opinions about how their partner should look. Once, early in my career, the male partner insisted that his Latinx female partner needed to be very blonde, and she couldn't contribute much during the consultation without him interjecting. He didn't care about my thoughts on what this would do to her hair or even how realistic that shade was based on her natural hair color. On a similar theme, I've had parents of young adults not allow their young people to contribute to the consultation on the outcome of how they would look. Early in my career I didn't know how to handle these, now I feel better prepared to read these situations and know when I can push back a little to encourage the client to have a voice. I am sensitive to not wanting to potentially contribute any issues for the client if this unhealthy or abusive person is present.

It's not uncommon for people to spend two to five hundred dollars on a custom color application and not want to spend thirty to fifty dollars on hair care to support their new look. This is hard for a few reasons, we can't guarantee our work without the supportive professional care at home, and we do appreciate it when you love the products we use, and you buy them from us versus online or elsewhere. I have also learned to navigate awkward conversations with clients about their hair during the service.

Love bombing and backhanded compliments are a frequent occurrence. They often come in a variety of fashions and topics, like:

- Styling: "I love how you do my hair, and I trust you so much. Why are you curling it that way? I loved my hair last time."

- Cutting: While I'm cutting their hair, they remind me not to go too short.

- Color: "I loved my color. Let's do the same color as last time." Then they evaluate it in the mirror after the service, asking, "Does this look different? I loved my highlights last time, are you painting them differently?

- Price: "Everyone here is so nice, your salon is so cute, the prices seem high, this isn't the Four Seasons."

- Schedule: "It was hard for me to get on your schedule, you're busy these days, you must be doing well."

- "Wow, you're done already, that was fast!"

I have gotten better at not taking these personal and managing them with direct and kind responses. I tend to lead with a question, "Did you like your hair last time?" even if they already said they did—great, then I got you. "Do you have some questions I didn't answer in the beginning or have you changed your mind about something?" is often met with, "Oh, no, sorry, keep going." Before they get up, I always do a quick check in. "How does it feel? How do you feel?"

Over a five-year period, I had six surgeries that took me out of the salon anywhere from a week to eight weeks. I had clients send me sweet notes of well wishes, some had shared they were praying for me, some had food delivered to my house or personally made me food, boxes of treats with current magazines arrived, adult coloring books, books or their reading list were given, lists of hot new shows and soft things like blankets and robes came in all kinds of packages. These acts of kindness meant so much. It amazed me that our time together and our connection meant enough to them to express it in these ways.

People have shared their pregnancy news, that they lost their job, dropped out of college, or got the job and haven't told their partner or family yet. They have shared their baby's gender or name when it is still a secret. They've shared separations, abortions, if they are exploring their sexuality or gender and not yet told their loved ones and confided in me. The added layer to these secrets I hold, is that most of my clients are in a community somehow, kids in school together, co-workers, or their family or friends also come to me or my salon. I am a place where people get to try out how they might share big news or maybe they are testing the waters to see if they are met with judgment. It is safe with me either way.

I have had a mom drop her two under-eleven-year-old daughters off for their first hair color appointment and sneak off to happy hour, so the girls told us. We had to call her a few times to get her to return. When she did, I had to explain that an adult needed to be present, and she should have checked in with us before leaving them. I tried not to judge while supporting my frustrated staff working on these kiddos, and the anxiety of liability of having two curious kids who struggled to be still while having chemicals on their heads. Pro tip, salons are not babysitting services: Always check with the stylists about how to manage the bookings.

I've heard countless dating stories, from apps to blind dates and professional matchmakers. The wild ones can be fun to hear, but I have had countless ones that have led to long partnerships and marriage. I love cheering people on in the quest to have the life they desire, including love.

I have heard horrible stories of how families are navigating domestic violence in their homes or their adult children's homes. I immediately work on my self-talk and putting on my armor, thank you to my therapist. I tell myself as someone who has been a child in this kind of home, I am only an expert of my story, I am responsible for my triggers and not to over share or advise. I do offer resources locally if they are open and looking for help.

I've had someone in my chair share her plan to take her life. While her color was processing, I was able to call my husband, who's a mental health professional, and asked for support on what I should do. If you ever find yourself in this situation where someone confides this to you, there are countless resources online and hotlines if you don't have access to a mental health professional immediately like I did. In this case, she got help and didn't take her life. I continued to see her for a few years until she moved out of state. I still think of her and hope she has a community supporting her and reminding her about the value she brings to the world.

I've had people share their addiction stories or spouse's addiction stories and the impact on their families, as well as parents struggling to support their children with addictions. Another one that requires me to put on some armor and make sure to only be a good listener, to remind them they aren't alone and offer resources if they need them.

I have had women with grown children share that they wish they never got married or had children. They were a generation when they felt like they didn't have choices, it's what you were supposed to do. We talk about the shift for women since their time and how important it is for choice. No matter if it's motherhood, career options, or choosing not to marry.

I have had men and women weep because having a child isn't happening for them. I grieve with them, there are no words, just whatever they feel is okay!

I've had people share horrible experiences of hate crimes against themselves or family members because of their race and sexuality. Yes, even in Seattle, which seems to be shocking to some. This has taught me, no matter your city or neighborhood, there are kind and hateful people everywhere. I have learned not to assume anything about someone based on a political leaning, beliefs, or what seems to be an inclusive message, and that people are having a variety of experiences, and to believe them.

I've had people trust me as they are transitioning genders to help them define their new look. I've had parents come to me with their young people who are questioning their gender and ask if I can help them experiment with their hair. This takes courage and vulnerability, and I am honored when anyone has considered me to be a safe space to explore their identity.

I've shaved countless people's heads and done home visits for people who are unable to get out of their chairs or beds due to illness. When things are out of control, it helps to have a haircut. You might not know this feeling, and hopefully maybe never will, so it could seem silly or weird to you, but when you barely recognize yourself it can really help. It can also just be about connection, self-care, or touch that isn't painful. It means as much to me to be invited in knowing you aren't mentally or physically who you want to be.

I've shared my time and talent with people who escaped domestic violence and people who are experiencing homelessness in shelters or hotels, organized by a nonprofit. These populations are vulnerable and brave to allow a stranger to touch them and possibly change how they look. Asking permission from them before touching, offering self-care, and having a say in something is empowering if you haven't had it in a while, or ever. I have said throughout my career this work for me has always been more than doing good hair, it is healing through touch.

RACISM AND RACIAL BIAS COMMENTS

I was asked by a white woman: "Do you think black women are jealous of white women's hair?" This was in 2019. My response was along the lines of, "No, I don't, and there is beauty in all textures and expressions of hairstyles." There is cultural pride in hair and texture, and the way people choose to style their hair can be a celebration of identity.

A black woman, and a friend, shared that, while working at a local university in Seattle, she was told her hairstyle was not appropriate for work, that it was unprofessional. This was the early 2000s, and at the time she was wearing her hair natural, meaning her curls and texture were free to flow. She did follow their recommendation and opted for a braided look for work in order not to receive any future action. As a society and in the hair community, we have a lot of work to do in this area. My question and belief around this is, "How is it ever okay to say how the hair someone is born with, or their chosen style, is any less professional than any other style? Policies or comments such as these are rooted in racism and bias.

I have had people come over when I am working on a different texture of hair and ask questions like, "How do you wash your hair?" Or even reach in to touch someone else's hair. As an educator, I welcome curious, kind questions and welcome opportunities to help people gain knowledge. As humans with our own limited exposures, it is important to find spaces to ask questions about any subject. As a stylist, I want to make sure the person in my chair feels comfortable, and if this conversation is welcomed. Sometimes, knowing my client, I just shut down the conversation from continuing, or I ask for consent to offer a teaching moment, and I have had times when my client has offered the teaching moment. When it comes to someone leaning in to touch someone else's hair, I turn into a security guard and have put myself in between to stop it from happening or a hand up to say no. It is never okay to touch someone or their hair without permission. I have had to do this at the salon and out in the world on behalf of friends and family, even most recently. I will say it again for the people in the back, it is never ok to touch someone else's hair without permission.

During COVID and the Black Lives Matter protests, I had a white woman in her seventies share while getting a haircut that she asked her girlfriends if they knew anybody that was racist like the news is reporting. Her and her girlfriends felt strongly that it was an exaggeration in the media that Black Americans were experiencing the hate that was claimed. I asked if any of those friends were Black women, they were not. I mentioned that could be a good place to start, by asking people you know, who don't look like you, what their experience is. To have a child like curiosity and trust what they are sharing. Many people know people from other races, religions, or LGBTQIA—that doesn't mean they consider us a safe space to have these conversations, so I offered that too. If you do have a diverse group in your life and they aren't sharing their struggles, there could be a reason, and it's not that they aren't experiencing it. I shared that people in my life, my family, have experienced hate and it was real and true for them. I tried to be kind, hold my value for others and plant some seeds. I wish I could say this was a one time conversation, unfortunately many versions of this have come up throughout my career, and I am still practicing the art of it.

I've heard people ask my co-worker, who was a woman of color, "Is that your real hair?" many times. She navigated it with grace and it didn't rattle her, often meeting the question with a joke or question back, "Is yours?" She worked on predominantly white women and I'm sure learned strategies throughout her career by the time I had met her.

Someone said to me, not knowing I had mixed-race children, that, "It must be sad for kids who are mixed and have their nonwhite parent's hair." As a professional and as a mother, I know any race, or mix of races, has a vast range of options for texture, density, and hair color. I was able to offer that as a teachable moment while sharing again that hair is a celebration of identity for many no matter the race. I can approach these questions when I hear the curiosity without stigma or judgement, and my answers vary depending on what I am met with, to be honest. I am a human, so sometimes the response can sound like, "Never thought of that, I'll ask my kids if they wish they had different hair." You can imagine the subject has changed.

As you can see, some of these are more specific while others are themes of conversations had multiple times. The human experience can be so complicated and surprisingly simple: We all want to be heard, valued, and some genuinely want to learn. Some people confide in or ask questions of their stylist, waxer, or bartender because they don't have someone else too.

I share these clients' stories as human interactions, as a tribute to the deep connections and responsibility of your service provider. I have been tested, offended, learned, and been loved so much through these almost thirty years. People, some strangers, have healed parts of me I never imagined could be possible to heal. I have also been imperfect these past thirty-ish years, making bad jokes, touching nerves, and making comments from a place of ignorance regarding race, religion, politics, and about marginalized groups. I'm still learning how to sit in the lesson while continuing to be a student of people and different experiences. I try to extend that same grace to others. I appreciate the opportunity to do better, and the chance to apologize with a change of behavior and my commitment to gaining knowledge. To me, a safe space means we come in with a teachable spirit and the ability to hear someone else's experience and accept it.

What is your favorite part of getting your hair done?

"My favorite part of getting my hair done is seeing Annie and connecting with her. The hair part is always fantastic, and I feel amazing every time I leave—in how I look with my fresh hair as well as how I feel, mentally too, as spending time with Annie always makes me feel better. Annie is truly a wonderful human being who also happens to be an amazing artist. The human aspect of her is what I look forward to seeing every five to six weeks . . . she has a huge heart, and I am lucky to have her in my life.'

—SIMMI B.
Seattle, Washington

"My favorite part of getting my hair done is talking with you! My stylist knows me better than any bartender. I love sharing stories about our personal lives every few months—it's a unique form of connection. Someone I don't typically see in my "everyday" life but who knows me and my family so well. And of course a secondary benefit of knowing me is giving me great advice on my cut and styling—what's going to work for me and my lifestyle."

—HILLARY M.

"Your hair is so crucial to your confidence. I won't even clarify that any further—
women, men, young, or old—the way your hair falls on any day can dictate a lot
about your mood. And while for most of my life I've "hated" my hair, felt it to be
unruly and uncooperative, I have to say that despite those feelings I've always
used my hair to exercise my independence and control. It's a time and place
when I have full decision-making power and am free to act on impulse or whim.
So, my favorite thing about getting my hair done is feeling empowered to do
exactly what I want.

—GEORGIA J.
Austin, Texas

CHAPTER 7

SALON OWNERSHIP AF

The Asymmetrical Cut: An *asymmetrical haircut* is a style where the hair is cut differently on each side, resulting in an uneven or nonsymmetrical look. This can involve variations in length, layers, or even distinct styles on each side.

It is a versatile hairstyle and gender-neutral. Usually it is a combination of two separate styles, one for each side. This haircut can be used to balance out the lack of symmetry in someone's face or just as a style choice.

This haircut perfectly describes salon ownership for me! It looks cool and can be perceived as edgy to an outsider. But to the owner, it can also feel weird or lopsided at times and can be hard to manage during horrible growth periods.

MY OWN PLACE

Some people start their career in the industry thinking they will be a salon owner one day. That wasn't the case for me. I had no lofty dreams of owning a salon or managing people. I loved working behind the chair, teaching, and mentoring, while letting somebody else manage the day-to-day responsibilities that come with running a business. It wasn't until I spent several years working under different leadership styles that I started to realize it was time to create the environment in which I wanted to work. By no means is this to say I was unhappy at every place I ever worked; it is simply proof that not one single place had all the elements I desired. I worked for a couple of great leaders, but their location or business model wasn't allowing me to grow at the pace they had promised. I worked in a couple places that had great locations but the leaders lacked vision or had poor communication practices. I worked at salons that were bustling with new clients but had toxic leadership. I noticed through the years that salons were owned or run by men while women outnumbered them as service providers and clients. So, I decided, it was time to start dreaming about what this potential salon could look like, feel like, and most importantly, how I wanted to run it. *Can I find this in Seattle or is it time to bring my concept to life?* I wondered. A woman-led, kindness-over-ego-focused salon that would allow driven creatives to showcase their talent.

I've become a firm believer that when you have a new dream or goal, you need to keep it close and protect it like a new baby. I am currently practicing this motto as I write this book. Only a handful of people know about this project. While I appreciate honest feedback on my big ideas from those who traveled the road before me, I've learned through the years that sharing my goals or new, big ideas with others gives them permission to project their own fears and personal experiences onto me. I just need to make sure my voice is the loudest in my head before sharing it with other voices. So, when exploring a new idea, I tend to find a small group of people with specific expertise to advise and guide me. I learned this lesson when I decided to stop going to college and begin my training at beauty school. Friends and family questioned if it would be a career that would allow me to provide for my family; they didn't see how it could provide the same security as a four-year degree. Well-meaning friends expressed doubt and fear as I shared with them that I was considering an out-of-state move. I learned quickly through that process, that if I was going to get where I wanted to go, I was going to have to stop sharing what I was exploring, until I had become clearer on how I was going to get there. Sharing the journey with others was no longer serving me, and so sharing the thought-out plan with confidence became my new strategy. As a classic overthinker, it was all so overwhelming, receiving so much unsolicited advice, opinions, and worst-case scenarios. But, no matter how many people tried to dissuade me, I just couldn't get the thought out of my head: *But what if it works?* A few years ago I read *The Subtle Art of Not Giving a F*ck* by Mark Mason and an idea Mason wrote about stood out to me: There's no such thing as a problem-free life, that every choice has a different struggle. This really resonated with me, especially reflecting on all the choices I've made—none was without struggle. Mason's idea also aligned with my motto: It's always a yes until it's a no, meaning if I can't let go of an idea, I will continue to work out all the pros and cons until I have a clear answer. Ultimately, the ability to move forward with an idea inevitably leads to the question: Is the risk worth taking or can I live with myself if I don't take the risk regardless of the outcome?

My first step into ownership was becoming a sole proprietor by leasing a chair at a salon. This business model allowed me to have more autonomy in the way I defined professionalism. I got to choose the services I wanted to provide, products I wanted to use, the schedule I worked, and the amount of time I wanted to take off without asking permission. I had to learn how to do bookkeeping, manage a budget differently, inventory, and understand the numbers part of work in a way I had always defaulted to my leadership. Figuring out how much it would cost me to provide a service, pay my salon rent, pay for my health care, cover my time off, and pay myself while maintaining my life was no small feat. There were many hidden fees in this process, like additional licenses I needed to have, additional insurances I needed to purchase, and the cost of products was a shock. I was warned by some stylist friends on how easy it is to get behind in your taxes and how hard it could be to manage all these logistics as a creative. Again, I knew this new chapter would come with different struggles, but I didn't think of them that way. To me, they were challenges, and I was ready to see if I could do it.

The salon I picked to have my chair in, turned out to be a supportive environment that helped me navigate all these new changes and responsibilities. I loved independence and many of my clients followed me to this location. I was able to grow my clientele with referrals from my existing clients, I still had room in my schedule to take overflow within the salon and people from the neighborhood who were reading our positive reviews.

After two and a half years of struggling in Seattle professionally, I finally felt like I had hit my stride. Over the course of the first year of renting my own chair, I was able to play catch-up and started to feel like I could rebuild my savings so I could breathe easy again. It was a few years into this new professional endeavor when I started to dream about owning my own full-service salon. I had learned how to manage myself and all these new tasks, while creating a big demand in my business during a recession, no less. My kids were getting older, I had a supportive partner at home, and I had things I still wanted to contribute to my industry.

I started to consider what it could be like to have my own space: Could I really be a salon owner? This process started with talking. More precisely, I talked the idea to death with my husband. He is a safe space for me to be a dreamer and to express my insecurities. After all the talking, it was time for some action. I knew I needed to learn more about running a business and the legal responsibilities of having employees, as well as learning about start-up costs. It was important to me to enter this chapter without compromising myself as a creative person, but also to be someone who understood the business inside and out. I returned to therapy to unpack a bit more of my stuff; I knew I wanted to be emotionally ready for leadership. I took classes in business management from salon owners who shared how they started their business. My takeaway from these initial classes was that the first step would be to write a business plan, develop some kind of employee manual, and get clear about expectations of the salon culture I wanted to create. It was fun to put this dream into something that I could see; I was amazed at how big it would be, and I loved picking out the products I would use and imagining all the types of people who would work there. The process also included meeting with a few other types of professionals who specialized in marketing and real estate to help inform my decision on whether I would move forward or not. I was lucky to have a couple of salon-owner friends that trusted me, and with whom I trusted, to have honest conversations about what this journey was really like. There is a lot of gatekeeping in the salon space, whether it's regarding techniques or how people run their business. I really appreciated those who shared so freely, and I continue to do the same; I am an open book when it comes to my wins and losses.

A couple of key takeaways I gained were not surprising; managing creative people and keeping them engaged can be hard. It's hard to make a profit, and size matters when starting out: too big means operating cost can kill you and too small would mean I would have to do a lot of the roles myself. I appreciated the candid conversations and took to heart their lived experiences. I'm not going to lie, it scared me. But here I was again. I had an idea I couldn't let go of, or rather, an idea that wouldn't let go of me, and I was going to have to do it afraid.

Overall, I spent two years doing my research. I knew I couldn't rush the process if I was going to do a thorough job of figuring out if this was the path for me. During this experience of exploring, I didn't share my findings with my clients because I didn't want to take them on the ups and downs of my journey or feel added pressure if ultimately my choice was not to move forward. I knew once

I had a concrete direction I would have a lot of support from clients. But, I just didn't want to take people along with me on my emotional rollercoaster.

As I was developing my employee manual and considering what kind of salon culture I wanted to establish, I was fortunate enough to have a lot of great mentors, educators, and personal experiences to pull from. I started to reflect on some of the toxic experiences I had been through and reframed them as an opportunity to address how I would handle those situations myself, should they arise. I also had so many positive experiences to pull from as well, and I saw them as an opportunity to consider the likelihood of those. I had mentors in the early days of my apprenticeship who knew that I was a single mother who didn't always have the resources and, after long days going from the salon to class, would offer to buy me a meal from time to time. I had kind and honest teachers who found me inspiring and allowed me to shine. I had mentors who made me question if I had any talent at all. I needed to learn how to be honest, kind, and inspire others.

When I was starting out in Seattle, I quickly decided the amount of notice I would give when leaving an employer, as well as how I went about giving that notice, which was based on the respect and safety that I felt under their leadership. When I saw a pattern of aggressive behavior from an owner, I left my note or resignation in her mail slot at the end of my workday and I never returned. One owner I worked for would regularly make other stylists cry while they were working on models or in his coaching meetings. His reactive delivery to me, when calling

out a mistake was a clear sign it was time to leave. I offered this salon owner two weeks' notice, and let them know I was happy to leave immediately, and he allowed me to just leave. A couple of times upon needing to hand in my resignation, I was overwhelmed emotionally with gratitude and conveyed my appreciation for the opportunity at their salon. It was an act of true self-love to state that I needed to leave because that was what was best for me. Many of my former mentors and employers have remained in my life, because leaving my position with integrity and respect for their businesses has always been important to me. So, even in some of the uncomfortable, or what I would consider toxic environments, I took those experiences as an opportunity to learn a lesson, and I took ownership of how important my personal exit timing was.

Once all my creative concepts, business plan, and preferred salon culture were clear to me, the most logical starting place was to find the part of town that I wanted my business to be in. I had learned from my previous moves that the further I went from my current location the less likely my current clients were to follow. Keeping that distance in mind, and with the hope to improve my personal commute home, I found a neighborhood that had high traffic and retail space available. I also knew I wanted to be near other complementary businesses like spas, clothing boutiques, and cafes. Something I've remained consistent in is my deep belief that there are a lot of ways to do hair, so other salons present in the area didn't deter me. I still believe in collaboration over competition. My dream was to create a professional environment where salons in the neighborhood could do classes together and refer clients to one another in the goal of building community over competition.

Once I found the neighborhood that checked many of my boxes personally and professionally, I decided to reach out to a woman who worked in a studio by herself and see if she would be willing to share her space with me while I was working toward opening my salon. I knew this would be a long shot, but I wanted to start our relationship off with transparency, which included sharing my goals with her, a little bit about where I had come from, and where I was going. She ultimately invited me into her space. I was so excited for the opportunity to settle my personal business and clients in the neighborhood I had envisioned. I shared my exciting news with existing clients as I invited them to follow me; I explained that this would be a temporary home because my goal was to eventually open a salon. I also took advantage of this time to start building relationships in the community and with other small businesses. My thought was that by being in the neighborhood I could also keep a pulse on the commercial real estate market, and check out space as it became available. Once I was a part of the community, people were more generous with information about the good landlords on the block or who to avoid; I was in the circle and it felt good! Some of this I went into strategically and some of this was a side effect of building relationships. Another benefit I took into consideration was the ease in which I could oversee construction when that time came if I was close by. I joined the small-business neighborhood group and started to contribute in meaningful ways from cleanups to fundraisers.

Opening up my own space required cash and financing. I assumed because I had been self-employed for several years leading up to this point, that it would be easy to qualify for a loan. I quickly learned I had no business credit built up and, just like our personal credit, having no credit is just as bad as having bad credit. No credit history makes it risky to fund loan applications, and so I was denied by several banks on any kind of traditional small-business loans. Again, I was faced with another door closing and had a choice: I could see this as a sign that this was not meant to be, or reframe it as an opportunity to get creative and make this dream happen. I got a business credit card immediately, and started building credit. Now it was time to find some money to get the rest of the project going. I had many big feelings of rejection, self-doubt, and shed many tears along the way.

My big feelings about rejection eventually evolved into feelings of amazement. I began feeling brave enough to share with a handful of people I trusted about the loan journey, and to my surprise, people started to offer me opportunities to partner or expressed interest in investing. The belief in myself that sprung up from those offers gave me the courage I needed to continue blazing my own path forward. Looking back, I can see that I needed the banks to deny me credit, otherwise I would have missed out on the vulnerability and love I experienced during this process. Ultimately, I had four investors agree to cover the start-up costs that enabled me to move forward on construction, the down payment on the lease, the salon equipment, and several other things I needed to get my dream off the ground. I hired a lawyer to put together loan agreements for each of my investors, which outlined the interest rates, monthly payments, the length of the loan, and a personal guarantee that their money would be repaid regardless of the success of the business.

I believe in hiring out for things that are not within my skill set, which is why one of the first people I hired for the construction of my new space was an architect who was also a designer. Together, we created a layout and picked out the décor, while maximizing the square footage. She took charge of securing all the construction permits needed from the city. I hired a website designer to establish my digital footprint and a contractor to finish the buildout and construction. When I first started looking for a space, I was hoping to find an already existing salon that I could just refresh to save money on the initial buildout. Unfortunately, there wasn't anything available, so I had to start from scratch. The most expensive part of building out a salon is making sure that the electricity is updated and able to handle our tools and lighting needs. The other high-ticket item to the budget when planning for a construction is plumbing—running water lines for laundry, shampoo bowls, a break room, and the color bar.

My first salon was 1,200 square feet, our lobby had many windows which let in so much light. The salon floor space had plenty of windows too—it is so great to have natural light when doing hair color. We were able to fit eight stations and three shampoo bowls into the space. While construction was underway, I was busily working across the street but was able to run back and forth between salons in order to receive deliveries, meet with my contractor, and watch the progress of my dream coming together. Sometimes, I would hang out there at the end of a work day, take in the vision, basking in the excitement and nerves. I would pray over the space and the future people who would come in. I would speak my intentions out loud. This helped me feel grounded and release some of the anxiety building about the journey.

There are so many great TV shows that depict delivering the house that's been made over or opening a business where you see the team working up until minutes before they hand over the keys to the owners and everybody's running around like crazy. It was exactly like that as we got closer to opening day. Shelves were being stocked, stations were getting wiped down, and windows were being washed until the very first person walked in the front door. We couldn't move in this space until the contractors were out and the inspections were finished so that meant all the finishing touches happened the night before and the morning of opening. We had a small team to open, products were stocked, stations were ready for bodies. A crucial part of running a salon is being able to shampoo people and our shampoo bowls didn't arrive in time. Day one we opened with holes in the ground with water lines popping up through them where shampoo bowls would eventually live. I found a portable shampoo bowl online that allowed us to take clients, but it also meant every shampoo required two stylists. One stylist was doing the shampooing, while the other stylist held the two separate lines of hot water and cold water, never achieving a balance. This process went on for a few days before our shampoo bowls arrived. I share this as a reminder that even with all the planning, and no matter how far in advance you order things, some things will require you to be flexible and pivot.

This flexible mindset applied to hiring too. I hired a green stylist and spent weeks training and onboarding them leading up to the opening. I had to let her go within a month of opening. It was my first time firing someone, and I was so scared to do it. But, I had a deep understanding that if the fit was off now, it would only get worse. By fit, I mean the things I couldn't teach. She was open to learning about hair but not so open to getting on board with salon culture and my definition of professionalism. I had a salon coordinator that I had onboarded, trained for weeks and did her hair so she could experience the services we would provide, but she gave notice a couple of weeks into opening. There was no easing into my new leadership role. I was working behind the chair four days a week, averaging one hundred fifteen clients a month. At the same time I was teaching classes with the staff, covering the front desk shifts as people called out, and doing all the owner's things like taking inventory, managing payroll, and communicating with clients and staff.

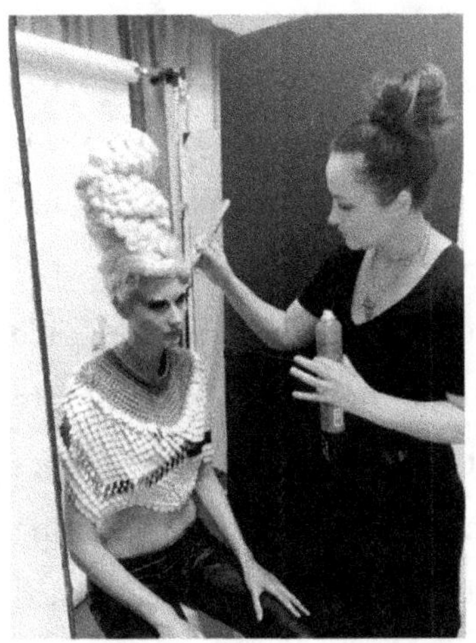

One of the most important lessons I gleaned from my mentors in years past was that I can't do more for someone than they are willing to do for themselves. I could certainly invest my time and energy into customizing an outline for my employees' success plans, but in the end, if they did not take the action steps toward their goals, that was on them. This was another teachable moment in being reminded that there is no such thing as a motivational talk or speaker, you are someone who comes in motivated and possibly gets inspired, or you are someone who hears something inspiring and changes nothing. Sometimes, I can spot this quickly and sometimes

I have to wait out the patterns in behavior to learn if someone can be inspired to make changes or just see if their actions and words match. We all know those people in different circles of our lives who talk about their goals and plans for success. Whether it's diet, fitness, reading more, or work related. I know, now, to listen for specific, measurable things in these conversations, because it gives me a clue that they are more than dreaming about a goal but haven't considered what it actually takes to achieve it.

So an employee working who struggles with time management, yet they don't see their pattern of how they get behind or how to catch up during a day or even understand the importance of communicating when it's happening so others can help. It has been my experience that this person, even with a thought-out plan of support and hype on how their day could be more profitable or how client retention could improve, won't be inspired or motivated to change because of their lack of ownership or awareness of their behavior. Consistency with a teachable spirit in any practice is the most uncelebrated and critical part of success, mastering something, and reaching a goal.

*　*　*

Was I overwhelmed, vibrating high, loving it, and wondering what I had just done to myself? Absolutely freaking YES! The part of me that felt comfortable in fear, anxiety, and stress was still not completely healed so survival mode on some level was still familiar and comfortable. I used to say I was just great at multitasking; I know now it was a deep need to people please, served up with a side of overthinking and trauma. The personal work I had done before opening my salon, I was about to discover, was just the intro course. Over those first few years, I strengthened my leadership muscles as I learned to hire slowly and fire quickly. I learned how to identify when someone was contributing to a toxic environment or if a new hire was simply not coachable. But the most critical lesson I learned that I keep with me still, is that the cost of keeping a person around is way more damaging and permanent than the temporary discomfort I experience when letting them go. If action isn't taken swiftly, you risk losing the trust and respect of your team. When my first couple of stylists decided to leave, it was a real gut punch. It felt personal. I had cared for and about them, and had invested in them accordingly. I was hurt, but recognized I had an opportunity to be the leader I said I would be. I didn't want to be a gatekeeper. If clients asked where a stylist was, I made sure that my team and I shared with the client exactly how to find them. If I was really going to practice this abundance mindset that I so often would talk about, I had to trust it. I regularly remind myself: *There's enough clients for everyone and there will always be new stylists excited to join our team and help us grow.*

I learned early on that people will leave—sometimes because they need to, and sometimes because you ask them to. What mattered most was how I handled those transitions and who I chose to be as a leader when they happened. When I first opened my salon, my goal was simple: I wanted to create the kind of place I would want to work in. I was a hairstylist first, and that experience shaped everything. I didn't want a salon led by ego-driven ownership. I wanted an environment where people felt respected, supported, and free to grow in a professional environment. That's why I realized the need to implement a system for healthy departures. It was an important part of the business plan I didn't have in place. At my core, I wanted for my team to know I didn't "own" them—or their clients. Instead, I built a respectful formula for how to leave well. Whether someone quits, is let go, or moves on to their next chapter, I do my best to support the transition—not just for the stylist, but for the client too. If I need to fire someone, I make sure their clients feel cared for, not abandoned. And trying to hold clients hostage only damages trust. At the end of the day, people have the right to choose who they want to do their hair—and I honor those relationships, even when they move on.

Over the years, this approach has produced surprising ripple effects. Stylists that moved on from us have referred us to their clients when they went out on maternity leave, or the clients return to us because they trust our culture. When a former team member retired, we were grateful to see some of their longtime clients come back through our doors. By not forcing relationships and choosing to support each individual's journey—whether it's an apprentice, stylist, or front desk team member—the side effect has shown that I've built something that lasts longer than just a single transaction. Sometimes that meant facing staffing gaps or temporary challenges. But the return has been priceless: genuine, long-term relationships with people who know they were seen, supported, and sent off with care.

I started my salon running like a large corporate salon in terms of policies, structure, offering education, and hosting events. Through the years we planned fun team bonding events, inviting staff partners too. We attended a drag brunch, went on-site to do glass blowing, took a painting class, a cooking class, went on a holiday boat cruise, and enjoyed private dinners with a chef. These provided an opportunity to get silly together, try new things, and most importantly, see each other as human beings who were fun, not just co-workers that sometimes annoy us. While treating everyone to these experiences was expensive, it was important to me to show appreciation and create connections amongst our team. An added bonus to this was inviting partners to join as well, and allowing them to see us in all our creative glory.

In this larger corporate model, some of my ideas became outdated quickly; our world was changing rapidly because of social media, and the industry started to shift in response. Within the first four years of opening, I had to pivot many of my policies and ideas. The core values of the business didn't change, just some of the operation's expectations. I was advised to look at my business plan every year and consider it as a roadmap that should be occasionally refreshed. At the end of the day, we are still cutting hair with scissors, and our other tools, while they have improved over time, are essentially still the same. A blow dryer, brushes, and even our hot tools, while the weight or some of the materials have been improved, the need for our hands, wrists, and bodies to guide them have not changed. Heads are always going to be round(ish) and hair is always going to grow out of them in growth patterns specific to each person. The tricky part was growing a business in an ever-changing industry when the service needed didn't change. At the end of the day, the desired outcome for us and our clients was always the same: to be the best version of themselves.

The experience of opening my salon was not linear and there are many things I wish I had learned sooner. When you are running a small business it's like having a baby, no one will love it as much as you do. They simply don't care about its growth, reputation, and success as much as you. A small business will never allow you to go on autopilot; if you are not working in your business, you are working on your business. Businesses will always require well checks, updates, and possible changes to navigate market demands and financial fluctuations. It's another chance to lean into one of my favorite reminders: *casualness can lead to casualties.* When you're too relaxed or unclear as a leader, it can show up in all the wrong places—unmotivated staff, dissatisfied clients, a space that starts to feel stale, and eventually, a business that begins to atrophy. That's why it's so important to lead with clear core values. They give you structure—and from there, you can be flexible without losing your foundation.

In my first few years of ownership, I was energized by this new exciting chapter. But after a few years in, I started to experience some health issues. I'm not talking just your average aches and pains that come with the job, but potentially life-changing issues like product sensitivities and allergies. Some of these medical issues required surgeries, sometimes with little or no notice, and they would take me out of the salon for weeks at a time. Again, this became an opportunity to learn, as I was reminded to trust the systems that I had created and the people that I had put in place to operate those systems. I continued to remind myself that my regular clients would be okay in someone else's chair once in a while, or perhaps, it was a great opportunity for the client to stay in somebody else's chair, but still within my salon. At my core I knew all these things to be true. Being forced into a situation by way of a medical emergency allowed me to lean on my team, ask for help and grace from my clients, and see that what I had built was indeed working.

These personal discomforts like pain, downtime, the recovery process, and the stress of rescheduling weeks' worth of clients coexisted with my gratitude for my team and my hope for returning to health. It was in the slow and quiet of recovery that I was able to reflect on my own personal happiness, survey my mental health, and measure my personal fatigue that ultimately allowed me to ask the hard question: *Do I want to keep going?* It's uncomfortable to work so hard toward the goal and then find that on arrival at said goal, you are wondering if you really want to be there or if the cost is just too high a price to pay.

Leadership stretched me in ways I never expected—not just professionally, but emotionally and physically. What a privilege to be able to explore this opportunity! My heart was heavy, my body was exhausted, and my doctors were making it clear: what I was doing wasn't sustainable. After many heartfelt conversations with my partner, I realized it was time to make a change. I needed to pivot—again.

Time to come up with another thoughtful plan; so we called a team meeting. It was nothing out of the ordinary. We ordered pizza like we always did. But this time, I cried my way through the conversation, big ugly tears and lots of nose blowing. I told them the truth: The current business model wasn't working anymore—not for the salon, and not for me. If we were going to continue being successful in the way I originally envisioned, I'd need to step away from working behind the chair and take on more of a managerial role.

And in that moment, the decision became crystal clear: I didn't want that.

I learned along this journey that I preferred working with clients over managing people. I love the connection, the creativity—not the constant policing of staff. So I shared a new, thoughtfully crafted plan with my team. I wanted them to know that as I explored a different direction, they had choices too.

Option one: They could join me at a new location—a salon I hoped to purchase—that would operate under a different business model, one offering more independence and personal responsibility.

Option two: If they felt called to pursue other opportunities that better aligned with their personal goals, I would support them fully. I promised to do everything I could to help them transition smoothly, including helping their clients follow them.

We agreed to keep the conversation in-house, giving each of us time to process and decide before making any public announcements. I was overwhelmed by the support, trust, and grace my team showed me at that moment. I knew they were scared and uncertain too—but we were navigating it together.

Most of the team chose to come with me to the new space, which I was able to purchase. A few decided to take different paths—and I respected that completely. Through this transition, I saw how deeply my people-pleasing tendencies had woven into every part of my business. I was terrified of letting anyone down. I seriously considered staying in a model that was breaking me—just to avoid disappointing others.

But I had a hard conversation, and got really vulnerable. I took the next step—afraid, but clear.

In many ways, it felt like leaving behind my "mothering" era and stepping into a "cool aunt" era. I still cared deeply, but I understood that it wasn't all my responsibility. This new model gave everyone more choice: stylists could lease a chair or work on commission as contractors. Either way, they would need to be more engaged and proactive in shaping their own success. And so would I—just in a different way.

It took four months to go from the announcement to the actual changes. I reached out to a broker, and she listed my current salon for sale. As a reminder I did not own my first space, but what I did have was the value of the salon build out and a negotiated lease to use as leverage. This broker knew other salon owners in the area who were shopping for bigger spaces or others who were looking to downsize their larger salons. Several people toured my space, and a nearby salon wanted my location. This sale gave me the opportunity to have a down payment on what became the commercial space that I purchased. If you've ever bought a home, you know it's always easier to buy your first because when you buy for the second time, this strategic planning of selling the first and closing on the second is much harder. The new owners who purchased my space were an amazing pair

of humans and worked with me as my timeline changed a couple of times due to construction delays (Thank you Alexis and Emily!). I did get lucky the new space had previously been a salon; the benefit of having the plumbing upgrades already finished was nearly priceless. However, the new space hadn't been updated since 1985, which was over thirty years!

The salon space I purchased had a legacy of its own. The previous owner was a beloved career hairstylist and a cherished member of the community who had passed away unexpectedly. His sister, who managed his estate, was the one who sold the property to me. I felt deeply honored to carry the torch forward—to continue the space as a salon and

preserve the spirit of what he had built. In my redesign, I included subtle nods to him as a tribute, small touches that honored his presence and legacy. Chris's Hair Collective became home to AFH Salon.

As I reflect on this process, I can't help but mention something that's obvious to those who know me; everything I do has to invoke a feeling, and it must be heart led. So, from salon culture, hiring and even the physical space I was creating, I knew that I had to feel it in my heart and gut to know I was on track. My life has taught me to trust myself and I don't take that for granted. Some people call it intuition, or being an empath or highly sensitive. I would say yes, I am all of the above. I have learned to listen to this part of myself and to lean into it.

So, when I think about my years behind the chair, as an educator, as somebody who's worked on set, and as a leader of my own team, creating a safe and kind space for myself and others wasn't negotiable. I do have a heart to help and give back, so sometimes I have hired out of potential versus alignment and that occasionally results in a lesson instead of the right fit. I've decided I can live with that. All the choices that I made from trusting my gut or my heart, regardless of the outcome, became opportunities to grow and practice listening to my inner voice.

Like most people, I don't like not being good at things, and this entire journey was uncomfortable and still can be. What I know to be true is that the only way we can get good at something is through practice. I also used this season of growth to really reflect on what parts of this journey make me happy. I would ask myself, *What do I enjoy doing?* And just like I scaled down my service menu, I decided I had to look at ownership the same way. Thinking of it like the first time I cut a precision bob haircut: Yikes! It took forever and wasn't awesome. Or, when I placed my first highlights—they looked more like stripes. But oh my, look at me now in my flow! Leadership and understanding how to run a business is no different, it just takes practice. Just like I had to find my personal style as a creative, I have had to find my personal style as a leader.

Part of the apprenticeship curriculum I created came from this concept: Find the small things that work and repeat them. I have chatted with many owners before, during, and now as an owner myself, about the loneliness of leadership and the pressure to be positive. Leadership requires holding up a mirror to see the truth and sitting in the hard parts as we make decisions for the greater good, even when others can't see it. Ideally, you have to have the trust of your team so when heads roll or changes happen, they feel comfortable discussing it and trust that you know what's best. I would say this often to myself when raising my kiddos; if they like me all the time or if liking me all the time is my goal, then I am probably not doing my job. This became my mantra as an owner too; I had to be okay with not being liked all the time. That meant accepting that my role in other people's stories is up to them. In some stories, I am the villain, in others, I am the loving mentor, and then, in some very specific ones, I am the boss with high standards. I'm sure there are many stories I play a part in that I don't know about, and I am okay with that. I ruminate on the times my words and intentions didn't line up and when I didn't get the chance to correct it in that specific interaction. I just hope to do better when the next opportunity presents itself.

By all measurable standards, my original business model and salon was thriving. It was running as smoothly as one could hope, growing steadily, and hitting every goal I had set monetarily. On paper, it was everything I had hoped for. But there was this uncomfortable tension—the success was real, yet I didn't feel the way I thought I would.

Giving myself permission to make a change purely for me—for my own well-being, mental health, and quality of life—is getting easier. But the truth is, it still takes me longer to act on that kind of change than it would if I were doing it for someone else.

LESSONS + PRINCIPLES I STILL FOLLOW
Communicating Change Effectively
- When implementing a new idea, share it *4 times in 4 different ways*—your team needs time and repetition to absorb it just like you did.
- More specifically, I committed to sharing policy changes 3 times in 3 formats: in person, over email, and posted in the break room.

Be Proactive, Not Reactive
- I avoid responding in the heat of the moment when frustrated or angry.
- If I must respond quickly, I stick to facts and avoid words like always or never to keep the conversation grounded and present.

Be the Person You Want to Meet
- I show up as the stylist and teammate I'd want to work with, from the quality of work to the energy I bring into the space.
- I'm mindful of my impact—from how I clean up after myself, to how I speak, work, and continue my education.
- I don't ask my team to do anything I wouldn't do myself.

Take Ownership of Your Experience

- When I feel stuck, I ask: *What's my role in this discomfort?*
- If the environment or relationships can't be changed and I've done my part, it may be time to step away.
- I take full responsibility for my happiness and wellness.

Contentment vs. Constant Hustle

- I'm learning to celebrate milestones instead of racing past them.
- Hustle culture can be draining and unfulfilling—I now pace myself for the *marathon*, not the sprint.
- Enjoying the journey requires *intentional effort*.

The Power of Community

- I stay connected with peers at different stages of life: behind me, beside me, and ahead of me.
- Everyone has something to teach—experience isn't the only teacher.
- I've invested in paid coaching when needed for clarity on finances, scaling, pricing, and goal setting.

Choosing the Right Coach

- Be specific about what you need and ask the right questions.
    - Are they experienced in leadership or just selling advice?
    - Have they scaled a business themselves?
- Many programs are front-loaded with access, then shift to prerecorded content with minimal contact.

- I personally value conversation and direct connection in coaching.
- I've worked with coaches inside and outside the beauty industry to stretch my thinking and explore creative applications of my experience.

TANGIBLE TAKEAWAYS FROM COACHING

Inner Voice Work

- I named my inner voices to better engage with them:
  - *Lois* (my grandma B.) is my encouraging, honest inner voice.
  - *Doris* (my critical grandmother) is my inner critic, rooted in fear and judgment.
- Instead of silencing them, I "invite them for tea," listen, and decide how much weight to give each voice.

Owner & Leader Support

- I found comfort in connecting with other business owners about the loneliness of leadership.
- These conversations helped me feel seen and reminded me I wasn't alone.

Professional Skill + Pricing Updates

- I streamlined my color application techniques and improved time management.
- I learned to calculate dollars per minute and per hour and adjusted underpriced services.
- I reduced my service menu—dropped offerings I didn't enjoy or that caused physical strain.

Pricing + Tipping Philosophy

- I considered the hourly pricing movement—not for me.
- I switched to *inclusive pricing* (no tips) and received great client feedback.
- Clients now know exactly what to expect, and I feel more aligned with my worth.

Retail Modernization

- I embraced affiliate retail programs to reduce overhead and expand options. While offering a curated selection of best sellers at the salon for clients to take home.
- Clients can now shop online and get products shipped directly—a win-win.

Remaining Open to Change

- I've learned to embrace change as a constant. Being open to what formerly worked or was "right" can change.
- Multiple generations now work behind the chair—understanding their needs matters.
- Healing people are flexible people. I strive to stay in growth mode, knowing it's okay to pivot.

CHAPTER 8

THE HAIR AND NOW,
HAVE I LOST THAT LOVING FEELING?

An Afro: An *Afro* is a hairstyle and a haircut. It is characterized by a naturally curly or frizzy round shape into a full bushy form. It's often associated with Black hair, but can be achieved with any hair type that can be styled to have that specific curl pattern.

Key characteristics of an Afro: the hair is styled to create a large, cloud-like shape, full and round. The hairstyle relies on the natural curl and the texture of the curl along with the haircut shape. Historically significant, Afros have a rich history, particularly in the Black community, and have been a symbol of resistance and cultural pride.

This cut and style represents resilience, flexibility, resistance, softness, and strength all at once. As I reflect on my career and life I connect with this deeply.

WHERE DO I GO FROM HERE?

At this stage of my career I reflect on the significant impact of my health journey, while unpacking my mental health in a deeper way. The physical cost of the work I do has had me wondering where I fit in this industry and if I still add value. I put off writing this chapter for so long; the vulnerability of saying it out loud scared me. If this was a handwritten assignment, it would have been covered by my dried-up tears. So much of my identity throughout my life has been about my work and how I contribute to my industry; it's also been about my art. My work has allowed me to provide for my family, build a community I value, witness examples of healing, hope, and openness due to all the many different types of people I have met along the way. My professional journey has opened my mind in ways I could have never guessed and led to so many adventures I know I would not have experienced working in another field. I have loved the client relationships I have built; I have loved doing hair for most of my life and the thought of not being able to do this work is devastating. I always imagined leaving behind the chair because it was time to retire, on my terms. I never thought my body, and my health, would put a ticking clock on my ability to work. Maybe I didn't mentally go there because of the pressure to provide for my family for so long. At times, I didn't have the luxury of checking in on my physical or mental connection to my work; there was just the need to keep all the balls up in the air. So, it has been a wild love affair of nearly thirty years and maybe, there has been a sprinkle of toxic productivity.

Have you ever wanted to leave the industry and why? Did you leave? If yes, did you return to it?

"There have been times when I considered leaving the hair industry. In my early years, I struggled to build a steady clientele, earned very little, and faced financial challenges. Despite that, I loved doing hair, enjoyed being around my co-workers, and appreciated the clients I did have. It was my stubbornness and perseverance that kept me going.

This line of work can be physically demanding. Around twelve years into my career, I threw out my back badly and was out of work for nearly two weeks. I was in a lot of pain and worried I might need to find a different path. I even started taking college courses and explored other career options. But through that process, I rediscovered my love for doing hair. After taking some cutting classes and finding new inspiration, I decided to work for myself—and it was the best decision I ever made. I've never felt happier or more passionate about my career. Sticking it out and not giving up got me to where I am today, and I look forward to the future in hairstyling."

—KANE BOWEN, Seattle, Washington
Eighteen years in the industry

"I have wanted to quit the industry before. I have been doing a version of hair and makeup in Seattle for almost twenty years. Just like any long-term relationship the growing pains have been excruciating and destabilizing but also comforting and glamourous. When you work mostly alone it can be hard to know what the temperature on your field is—am I good at this? Am I relevant? I also think that when you work in beauty, you're never allowed to turn it off, everyone wants to look good and so anyone can talk about it. It's strange to be in an industry where you are both considered service and the help but indispensable to those you work on. It can be so fun to see how leveling it is when a very impressive person gets down to brass tax and just wants to be hot. It can hurt to feel invisible while at the same time holding all the best stories and dirtiest secrets. One must fight the ego for wanting to be seen by a client. The most seasoned artists I know tend to have a picture of how little these matter and see how beauty has never really been a deal breaker on whether a client is wonderful or worthy.

What brings me back over and over is when you do get to make someone feel worthy, feel themself. It's hard not to love the freedom of life and the potential financial independence of this job but you also never know what you are going to get, which can make it both the best and the worst."

—KAIJA MISTRAL TOWNER, Seattle, Washington

"Yes, many times! Especially when times got tough, such as the pandemic, and also when I had a bad day with clients and couldn't get anything right with their color or cut—just feeling like a failure and I should just give up and work at Starbucks. I never actually left because I love it so much! I literally LOVE everything about it, even when I'm having a bad day, one of my wonderful clients will walk in and we'll talk things out—hearing what they are going through and knowing I'm not alone is the best feeling. Also, when I nail someone's cut or color, the feeling is indescribable. It's the best! I love making people feel good. Probably the most surprising thing about being in this industry is discovering my underlying need to help people. I can't imagine doing anything else!"

—JENNIFER ALDEN, Glendora, California
Eleven years in the industry

"I did want to leave the industry about eleven years ago. I was at a salon that didn't inspire or motivate me, I felt stuck and was making little money. I went back to college online to complete a bachelor's in business so I could get a "nine-to-five job" while still doing hair during the day.

That salon abruptly closed one year ago before I finished my degree, so I decided to go independent and see what happened. From then on, I thrived. Entrepreneurship sparked something in me that I had been missing for the last few years. I loved doing hair again and, furthermore, loved creating an environment for my clients to relax in and enjoy. I've been independent for eight years now and feel more fulfilled in my career than ever before. I've built a strong business that I can be proud of, and I'm so glad I never left the industry that has given so much to me."

—MORGAN THOMAS, Wheaton, Illinois
Nineteen years in the industry

It was during the COVID closures that I really got the chance to take care of myself. It was the first time, even amongst the discomfort of everything going on in the world, that I didn't have kids at home to care for, and it was just me and my partner. Yes, I was anxious about the state of the world, my own underlying health conditions and the impact if I got COVID. There was much to consider and much to be afraid of; the financial impact on my business, grieving losses of people, and sadness when I couldn't gather with my family, as well as the constant worry I felt about the impact on my team. But for the first time ever, I had time to check in with myself, even though it was the isolation that forced it.

I took the time to consider how I wanted to return to work. We had just made the move into our new space and had only been open for a few months. What ended up being a three-month mandatory closure allowed everyone on the team to step up and manage their client inquiries and ultimately their own rescheduling for reopening, which was exactly what our new business model had been built around. During that time, I did some Zoom meetings with business coaches and trusted mentors to start the conversations, looking for my next step and support in how to let others step up. The physical rest and the quiet time allowed me the space to reflect on the last several years and dream a little differently about my future. I knew in the moment how lucky I was, and still think about how privileged I was during that time. I reflect on it as an uncomfortable, scary yet revealing gift the forced closure gave me.

In 2017, my commission salon was busy with a full team and we were thriving. I also started that year with an indescribable amount of pain in my abdomen and some other underlying symptoms that no one could figure out the cause of. I have a high tolerance for pain, but this discomfort was not manageable. After months of dealing with this sharp pain that would have me bent over and ultimately lead to throwing up, it was finally decided that my gallbladder needed to be removed. It took several doctors' appointments and ER visits over the course of five months to confirm this.

My medical journey has unfortunately had a consistent pattern; my symptoms never quite create a clear diagnosis, and it requires a lot of self-advocacy to get there. Although the surgery recovery was harder than I thought it was going to be, I started to feel so much better, eventually. Unbeknownst to me, this would kick start an intense health journey that would force me to lean on my team and realize the success of my business was not completely reliant on my own ability to earn.

Unfortunately, after the surgery, I started the next year with a similar pattern—one of constant pain and a whole host of other symptoms. My journey with health has never been clear cut, so again, it took another several months of tracking intense symptoms because I wasn't a textbook case. It was decided by my doctors that I needed to have my appendix out almost a year to the date after I had my gallbladder removed. These first two surgeries were significant because it really helped me recognize existing gaps in my business; the necessity of letting go, permission to take care of myself, and the need for better health insurance. At this time, my partner and I had made the decision that it was cheaper for me to have my individual plan as a small business owner versus joining his work plan. But my out-of-pocket on these surgeries was over twenty thousand dollars each. So, after the second surgery, I joined his health care while recognizing I'm so grateful to have had any at all. I had enrolled in Aflac disability insurance some years before, and it was determined that I didn't meet the requirements to receive any coverage for these surgeries. The stress of growing my business, having kids in private school and college, and now back-to-back years of almost fifty thousand dollar hospital bills really stressed me out. Again, this was not the time to check in on my level of fulfillment and enjoyment of work; I simply needed to do more of it. Working as a stylist means if you don't work you don't make money, so unplanned time off can be tricky, especially when my income contributes to the business and home.

Over the course of five years, I ended up having six surgeries in total, some with little notice, and some were emergencies. I was out of work anywhere from one to eight weeks for recovery, and I spent tens of thousands of dollars on said surgeries. These years were a wake-up call in many ways; I needed to switch up my business model so I could lighten my own load.

I'm somebody who's always been hard on myself; I have a high bar for how I show up in the world and leading by example is important to me. I've been tired, sad at times, and because old habits die hard, I've fallen back into my patterns of suffering silently. The physical pain I was in would be so bad at times that I would pull my car over to throw up on my way to work, or take cover in the bathroom in between clients to have a good cry. I would always wipe my face, rinse my mouth out with water, and then slap a smile back on my face. I had made an agreement with myself to be a good leader and somehow, I had determined that meant I didn't feel pain or if I did, I couldn't show it. *WTF was that about?*

Okay, I know now why I did this, and so does my therapist. It took a while to figure it out, but what we determined is that I wanted to be aware of the energy that I brought into the salon, but that awareness took me to a place where I felt like I was going to break, and those I was supposed to be leading would find me crying in the break room because the pain and the emotional overwhelm had caught up with me.

I tried to communicate to my team a little bit about what was going on with my health and how hard I was trying to show up for them and my clients. I was acutely aware that I didn't want my silence to come across as though I was withdrawing from the team, but I also didn't want them guessing my state of mind. Then, as soon as I would go through the mental gymnastics of what I shouldn't say and how I should be acting, I would spiral into a deep, dark hole of shame and guilt.

I struggled with the belief that I was not being a good leader if I allowed myself to just be human. I didn't share any details with my clients about what I was going through, unless I had to reschedule their appointments for surgeries and then do the same for the multiple recoveries. I've learned to be more human, allowing myself to be a little less "perfect." This time allowed me to receive help in ways that I had only given to others. One of my stylists started a meal train when I was out for one of my longer recoveries, and the team, as well as friends from other salons, added my clients into their already busy schedules. I made it to the milestone of just over a full year without a surgery and somehow, I began to believe that one year was enough time to heal, and that I needed to shape up, be happy, and tell everyone I was fine. I had been going to therapy to process all I had been through and allowed myself to grieve about my illness, as well as the guilt about all the missed and cancelled plans. Unfortunately, that milestone would be interrupted as I ended up back in the hospital, just a few weeks after that milestone with what I feared was a heart attack. I couldn't breathe; it felt like something was sitting on my chest. My blood pressure dropped, and I was lightheaded. When I got to the ER, they treated my symptoms as a coronary event; a pulmonary embolism. So consistent with my previous health journey, it would be a mystery that would take months and many doctors, urgent care and ER visits, to get to the bottom of. Ultimately, I was diagnosed with adrenal insufficiency. It seemed my body was no longer making cortisol, a hormone that we need to live.

I learned what I had been having was an adrenal crisis— a life-threatening emergency from not having enough cortisol, which can lead to low blood pressure, low blood glucose, low blood sodium, and high blood potassium. It really did feel life threatening and scary, and it was so hard to put into words what I was feeling since I felt disoriented or sometimes winded. I also learned there was a treatment which would allow long-term management of my newly diagnosed disorder: hormone replacement therapy. This treatment would replace the hormones I was lacking and, while they definitely come with a variety of their own side effects, they have allowed me to avoid major adrenal crises so far. As I write this I'm still learning about this condition and how to manage it.

I started out 2025 mentally and physically struggling, trying to figure out how to get my mind around my new life and limitations. For most of my thirty-year career, I have worked four to six days behind the chair, taking on clients, and still conserving energy for other special projects I loved. I had the energy to give to my team, as well as sit on committees for fundraisers supporting causes I cared about, teach in my community, all while volunteering at shelters cutting hair a few times a year. All of these responsibilities, combined with maintaining my personal life, left me struggling with anxiety about whether I would be able to keep plans based on how I would feel the next day. My stamina has been greatly impacted by this condition, as well as my mental clarity. It is a weird place to be in having worked so hard to be exactly where I am and to have a salon with a full and very talented team . . . to now be working three days a week doing hair with a great clientele and struggling to have the joy (or to be honest, the energy) I expected to have at this stage.

I have made many lifestyle changes to support my health throughout the years and that continues to take place with each new diagnosis. I feel so fortunate for the privilege to have the resources I have so that I can afford the recommended supplements and therapies I need to get better. I sit in the frustration of navigating the health care system, sometimes feeling like I'm not being heard as I try to push through my days with the self-inflicted pressure to show up for others because I know I have more to contribute to the world. And I feel this pressure so acutely that at the last hospital run I asked my husband, who hadn't read any of this at that point, to promise me to follow through on getting it published if something took a turn for the worse. He is a good sport; he understands that I have experienced so much death in my life from an early age, and so it's important to me that the people who are the closest to me know my wishes if I should "go" first. I have many wishes, and now added to that list is to please share my words and voice, if for some reason I can't. I tend to live in a state of urgency due to the deaths I have experienced. I have to say "I love you" or that I am hurt or grateful, I must take chances, and I am keenly aware tomorrow isn't promised. Even most recently, after losing a couple of dear friends in their forties and having our final conversations seared in my heart, as long as I am able, I feel compelled to honor them by carrying on the lessons I learned from them.

I have heard many versions of this same story from others, and I believe it: Pain travels through families until someone is ready to feel it. For many of us, our generational curse is avoidance. We come from people who just act like it didn't happen, but pain demands to be acknowledged and felt at some point. I believe I am the child who was born with the charge to feel it. Most of us get labeled as being sensitive, depressed, anxious, or even as healers. I believe the pain that you refuse to feel can't ever be healed. At this stage of life, I am leading with my heart and vulnerability with less worry about the judgment and stigma—the weight has become too much for me to bear and has made me ill.

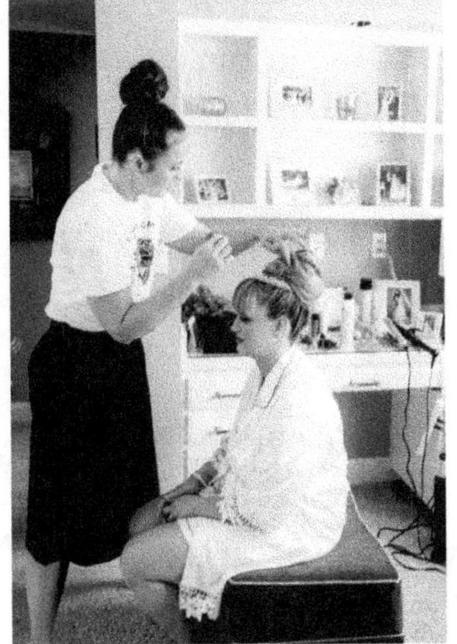

A wonderful side effect of all of this is that I can share my needs and truths a little more easily. In business, I am working on allowing less guilt about not being able to do it all, not saying yes to every client request, and having a manageable work day where I make sure to hydrate and eat during the day. As far as giving to my team, it is my spirit to be generous with my experience. I have learned to give as much as people are willing to do, coaching or sharing wisdom with people who aren't willing to put it into action will burn anyone out.

I get asked regularly by people who care about me, "Why don't you just stop working?" I choose to hear it as care, and it gives me an opportunity to educate them on what I have invested in my career, and that it is so much more than just a job. My skills don't transfer to other types of employment very easily, and my household relies on my income. It is hard not to get defensive, because sometimes, I still feel like the teen mom who was often counted out, like I couldn't be anything because beauty wasn't a real career. The assumption that starts these conversations is that my partner is the breadwinner or that my income doing hair couldn't be that big of a number to be a loss in our household.

My life hasn't had a lot of safety nets and in this season, I am playing catch up from years of making other choices, and prioritizing providing for everyone else. Whether it's food, housing, a paycheck, or a friendly and understanding work environment, I have done my best to be everything for everyone. But now, it's time for me. I have a business savings account for the first time, which means I can travel more and take time off, and I have been consistently contributing to a retirement plan.

Long gone are the days where I had to call family when my kiddo broke a tooth and I didn't have the money for the needed dental work, or rely on my local church group for Christmas gifts. Over the years, my relationship with money has had to evolve, as the mindset of scarcity has been replaced by allowing abundance into my life in so many ways.

These last two years, with this new diagnosis, have probably been the hardest years of my health journey to accept. All my other issues could be resolved with surgery or lifestyle adjustment, this one is one I will have to learn to live with, because there is no quick fix. I understand why my energy and my ability to vibrate as highly as I used to, have been so hard to sustain. I have said for years that our best is a moving target from day-to-day, but for me, that is still hard to accept. Unlike my other medical issues which required action rather than a lifestyle adjustment, this one has a lot of unknowns. I've been so hard on myself, questioning my work ethic and whether or not I even love my work anymore. *What's wrong with me?* is something I wonder about all the time. With the help of my therapist, and making the decision to cut back at work and getting quiet with myself, again, I sit in the belief that multiple things are true at the same time. I do love my work, I love the connection with the people who sit in my chair, I love creating and problem solving, I love talking business with other salon professionals, I love being a supportive team member, I love the feeling of being proud of my work, and I love owning a space that I'm proud of. What I don't love is working when I feel overwhelmed by my health journey, or feeling like I'm disappointing people because I must cancel and reschedule clients because I don't feel good. I don't love not being able to bring my best, biggest energy to my salon environment and being the hype-creative who energizes my team and my clients consistently. I don't love working when I'm in physical pain and how often I've had to. I'm so grateful for a career that allows me to make such a great living and build amazing relationships but the responsibility of it when I'm not well is difficult.

For the last few years, I've continued to invest in my craft as a litmus test. Do I still have what it takes? Do I still have the love and passion? I continue to take classes to learn new techniques, I keep scheduling meetups with other salon professionals and investing into business development. I keep waiting for something to click to reenergize me, when really, it's never been about needing more energy, it's been about needing true rest. I do want to keep working, creating and contributing to this industry as long as I can while working what that looks like now.

I'm a doer and my identity has been created around my ability to survive, multitask, and learn how to thrive. Somehow, throughout the course of this journey, I equated the need for cutting back on work and the tension of not enjoying work when I don't feel good as an indicator that I don't love it anymore. Granted, there are more days now when my pain is manageable and my energy seems to be good and I feel like I could conquer the world, my stamina is not the same. I've realized that no number of classes or community can make me love the work when I'm in pain and discomfort. This is a hard pill to swallow. The grief continues as I persevere to lean into learning how to be vulnerable while understanding that not everyone will understand my situation.

My team has experienced me being sickly in some way for a while, and I feel guilty about that while knowing it's not my fault. I feel guilt about all the appointments I've had to cancel. Personally, I had to cancel hosting our traditional Christmas Eve dinner and traveling for a dear friend's memorial. I have passed on gatherings because of feeling overstimulated and learning what spaces or group sizes feel more comfortable to be in. I have had to set more boundaries with friends and family on visiting or staying with me, and that has been revealing; my circle got smaller as a result. When I was unable to take care of others in the same way they no longer desired to have a relationship. On the other side of that a small group showed up and held space no matter how I was doing. I sat in knowing those were the right decisions and the grief of missing those moments and or people. I'm still struggling to accept or understand maybe even what my new normal is. I currently wear a medical ID bracelet in case I am unconscious, so the medics will know how to treat me. I take pills three times a day or more and keep a shot on hand for emergencies. I have had a lot of time to reflect at the end of the year and all the stillness, I realized just because I didn't have surgery doesn't mean it was an easy lift. I think I counted eight urgent care or hospital visits and one ambulance ride in 2024. I ended the year with almost as many unanswered questions as I started the year—and just as many upcoming doctors' appointments. It was kind of rare to go for a week or two with one this last year.

I've learned that it's no badge of honor to suffer silently; one of the unintended consequences of doing so is that the body can only stay in fight or flight for so long. You can only stuff so much trauma, pain, and unhealed versions of yourself down for so long before your body says, "Enough." The doctors still can't pinpoint exactly why my body, at this age and stage, is no longer making cortisol. I believe in the theory that the body does keep the score, and the years of survival have simply caught up with me. Let this be my PSA to unpack as you go, friends: It is never too late to start taking better care of yourself, and stress can be a silent killer, or at minimum, it leads to chronic illness.

As I cautiously move through 2025 with guarded optimism, for the first time, I'm not looking too far ahead. I currently struggle with making plans, not knowing if I'll be able to keep them and trusting that my now even-smaller circle of friends and family will understand that it's not personal; I'm not flaky, I'm just caring for myself. So far, not all have understood, and some have pulled back, including family, and I want to remind you to be ready for that. I have prided myself on being a reliable person, so this illness has forced me to be flexible with my definition of reliable. I'm grateful for the grace that some people have given me while being aware that people's empathy goes as far as their own level of understanding. For those who have never had surgery, it's difficult to understand somebody's healing journey. Or for those who have the kind of job that offers health care and paid time off, why would they understand the stress that comes when you don't get paid if you aren't working? It's weird to have an illness where you can look okay on the outside, but on the inside, you feel like you're short circuiting. My brain is foggy, my words don't always come out clear, my energy level is off, and I often feel overwhelmed and overstimulated when things are loud; I'm even more sensitive to people's energy. Salon days can be hard when the team is buzzing all around. It used to be the best feeling in the world, but now at times, I find myself wanting to hide, go for a walk, or just drive home in the quiet. I cry a lot more now, happy tears, overwhelmed tears, and streams of grief just pour out of me from time to time. I used to be embarrassed to cry or saw it as weakness, and now, it's something people would use to describe me. "Oh, that Annie, she's a crier!" and I am okay with that.

I don't know what this next chapter holds, but what I do know is that my hands hurt, and the arthritis isn't going to get better; that my product sensitivities continue to increase, which impacts my asthma and sinus issues; and that with my latest diagnosis, I don't know how I'm going to feel day-to-day. I do know that whenever my time comes to pivot, I want it to be known that I have so much love and respect for the work that I've created and the relationships that I've built. That I held space for others, offered inspiration, and was inspired by others, even as I hold space for myself, allowing an acknowledgement of how hard it's been.

I've heard it said many times by other creatives that so much beauty comes from our pain, and I feel like my life and my art has been a tribute to that. From how I was committed to breaking cycles in raising kids to being seen as a creative and professional, I have worked tirelessly to grow into a woman who speaks up while showing compassion.

Since learning about my latest condition, I have mentally tried on so many options. Should I work by myself? Can I still work? Should I be an employee somewhere and let go of all the responsibilities I have in owning a business? I do want to work; I have been the breadwinner for most of my life, and I have worked hard to maintain financial independence, and I still contribute to my household and its demands. My husband and I have worked tirelessly as a team to create the life we have along with some of its newly found comforts, and the thought of going back to living in financial uncertainty is scary. I keep telling myself it's okay to try on these options and not to make any decisions when I'm at the height of not feeling well. Unfortunately, I have yet to get a streak of feeling well so I continue to plug along, hoping for that moment of clarity. Meanwhile, my brain continues to dream up new business ideas and ways that I would love to support my team and their growth. I think about creative projects like editorial work or concepts for photo shoots, and even this project as I write and all the ways I would love to use it to connect and inspire within the industry. I know I'm not done yet—I just don't know how it's all going to fit together. It's yet another leap of faith and a practice in believing in the unknown. I believe this human experience of feeling your feelings while finding a way forward is constant and is truly the gift of being alive.

To close, I want to leave you with one last manta: In the words of the beloved Dolly Parton, "Find out who you are and then do it on purpose." Be uniquely you.

What would you hope people would remember about you, your legacy?

"I hope people remember that I was always learning alongside them. I aspired to be as creative as the young stylists I was fortunate enough to observe. No matter where you draw your creativity from—whether it's rooted in romance or innovation—what matters is that you remain authentic."

—NANCY ORTA, Tucson, Arizona
Over forty-four years in the industry

"I hope that people remember that I had integrity, I always wanted to leave people and things better than when I found them. I believe that if you put the hard work in, the sky is the limit. I hope that the education that I have provided anyone I have ever helped will live on through their work and their private lives. I love with all my whole heart."

—ALLISON EVERAGE, Lake Charles, Louisiana
Thirty years in the industry

"I want people to know how deeply I loved this industry. To me, leaving a legacy means inspiring the next generation. My legacy encompasses my roles as a stylist, business owner, and educator, but it goes beyond that—I genuinely cared about the people I worked with. I touched the lives of thousands, and I believe I not only saved some lives but also helped others recognize the true value of our industry, which is so much more than just outward beauty. I am passionate about sustainability and made it my mission to lead the industry in green practices. I was ahead of my time in modeling a salon that prioritizes eco-friendliness, and I was fearless in making changes for the better. I hope to be remembered as someone who not only embraced beauty but also championed a more sustainable and purposeful approach to our work."

—LISA VANN, Seattle, Washington
Thirty-seven years in the industry

"That I refused to be controlled—I charted my own course. That beautiful timeless, well-crafted hair always works. Gimmicks and trends don't. That whatever I achieve or have is mine—not my proximity to any person or product. That I dedicated my career to creativity."

—CHARLIE PRICE, Denver, Colorado
Thirty-eight years in the industry

"I would hope that people remember me for one thing above all else: that I genuinely cared. For my clients, I want them to recall feeling heard, seen, and truly witnessed during every appointment, every conversation, and every experience in my chair. My goal was always for them to leave the salon feeling a profound sense of peace, happiness, and renewed confidence.

For anyone I had the privilege to teach, whether in a class or through mentorship, I want them to feel that they gained actionable value they could immediately take home and apply to the real-life challenges they faced in their own salon businesses. My legacy isn't just about beautiful hair; it's about the positive impact I had on both my clients' well-being and my fellow stylists' professional growth."

—DELORA MAY DAY, Columbia, Missouri
Sixteen years in the industry

A PAGE FOR YOUR THOUGHTS

POSTSCRIPT

HAIR AND FAMILY

MY FAMILY AND MY CAREER WERE BORN TOGETHER; all those years ago I had to apply for that job at Glamour Shots for my family as much as for myself. Together we have shared this incredible journey as I've navigated my career, motherhood, and marriage. My children grew up watching me cut hair in our home to earn extra money, they would sometimes come to set and watch me prep models, asked to sweep or bring drinks and snacks to the team. In the later years it was my family who helped build furniture for the salon, worked at the front desk when I needed coverage and attended hair shows I was a part of. How could they not be affected by my passion, creativity, ambitions, tenacity . . . ?

I've learned and shared that being a hairstylist is demanding work—emotionally and physically—and being both a salon owner and hairstylist even more so. Your family comes along on this intense and amazing ride with you, and I wondered how my years, and decisions, in the industry affected those that I did everything for. So I asked. And I thought it would be appropriate to close with their thoughts—

Do you think watching your mom or wife pursue a creative career and build something as an entrepreneur has influenced how you see work, creativity, or even how you move through the world?

Roy (Husband): To a creative person, no doesn't exist. There's always a possibility. Historically, I've been more of a worker bee—tell me what to do, point me in the right direction, and I'll get the job done. Being married to someone with a creative mind and consistently being challenged to imagine beyond what can be seen has enabled me to expand my view of what is possible.

One of the greatest gifts of being married to someone with a creative mind is being challenged not to immediately say no to something but to wait and see if there could be an opportunity available. This shift in perspective has allowed me to slow down and take advantage of opportunities that I might have otherwise missed out on.

Taelor (Second born): Watching my mom build a creative career deeply shaped how I understand work, creativity, and purpose. She taught me that our value lies not in what we do, but in who we are—and that whatever we pursue, we should give it our full heart. She created space for exploration and self-discovery, encouraging us to color outside the lines to find our voice. I move through the world with patience, curiosity, and kindness because I watched her embody those qualities in all she did. I would always hear her say, "It's not just hair," a simple phrase that carries so much meaning. What may seem small, often holds the deepest significance.

Rob (First born): Short answer, hard yes. Since this is a book, whoever is seeing this already bought it and may be interested in knowing more . . . OR IS A THIEF. lol

Let me expand a little.

Growing up I didn't make the connection that hair is art, or at least can be if the right person is doing it. For a long time. It was just my mom's job . . . once I got a little older, I realized mum dearest was exceptionally talented and the opportunities she was getting was a reflection of not just skill she honed through dedication to her craft, but the ability to see a vision in her mind and execute. Combine this with her desire and need to provide for me and my little sister on her own, it became a fierce combination of work ethic, commitment to excellence, and creative genius. If you've seen her sculpt hair in person, or if you've seen a photo or video of the results, you know I'm not exaggerating.

Seeing your primary provider, caretaker, and biggest hero make a life through her passion for making people feel good, and look good too, is inspiring. With the flair and industry-recognized artistry she possesses, you can't help but wonder if your "dreams" can in fact come true. But dreams are just hopes until you take action. Her influence and the very intentional way she navigates the world has been the single most impactful example for me on my journey through life.

I was taught and shown it's okay to care deeply, so deeply it sometimes hurts.

I was taught and shown it's okay to show and express emotions, thoughts, ideas so big they may seem impossible until you break them down smaller.

I was taught and shown you don't have to do things a certain way "just because that's how it's always been done."

I was taught and shown that everyone deserves love no matter what their beliefs, self-identity, or preferences in a partner are, and this doesn't change the fact that they are a human sharing this world with us.

I was taught and shown how hard you must work to make a living, not just as a small business owner but also pursuing it through art.

Most importantly I was taught and shown what it looks like to hold yourself and others accountable. How to move forward with kindness and forgive even if undeserved. Set expectations and then be the example of excellence. I'm proud to say this has inspired me to become an entrepreneur with my own business in Seattle. I am setting a new standard for music industry events and artist management.

My mom is amazing, and I'm so proud to have been blessed with our life together to this point and moving forward. Growing, learning, making mistakes, and ultimately just developing our mutual understanding TOGETHER.

LOVE YOU MOTHER! KEEP UP THE GOOD WORK!

HELPFUL RESOURCES

PERSONAL

Below are some books that helped on my healing journey. There are too many to list, but here are a few of my faves:

Blowing My Way to the Top: How to Break the Rules, Find Your Purpose, and Create the Life and Career You Deserve, Jen Atkin.

Burnout: The Secret to Unlocking the Stress Cycle, Emily Nagoski, PhD, and Amelia Nagoski, DMA.

Girl, Stop Apologizing: A Shame-Free Plan for Embracing and Achieving Your Goals; Girl, Wash Your Face: Stop Believing the Lies About Who You Are so You Can Become Who You Were Meant to Be; What If YOU Are the Answer?: And 26 Other Questions That Just Might Change Your Life, Rachel Hollis.

Lighter: Let Go of the Past, Connect with the Present, and Expand the Future, Yung Pueblo.

Main Character Energy; Radically Content: Being Satisfied in an Endlessly Dissatisfied World; The Alchemy Within: Vignettes, Jamie Varon.

Running on Empty: Overcome Your Childhood Emotional Neglect, Jonice Webb, PhD, with Christine Musello, PsyD.

The 5 Resets: Rewire Your Brain and Body for Less Stress and More Resilience, Aditi Nerurkar, MD.

The Body Keeps the Score: Brain, Mind, and Body in the Healing of Trauma, Bessel van der Kolk, MD.

The Four Agreements: A Practical Guide to Personal Freedom, Don Miguel Ruiz.

The Givers and the Takers: Discover the ole You Play in the Dance of the Opposites, Cris Evatt and Bruce Feld.

*The Subtle Art of Not Giving a F*ck: A Counterintuitive Approach to Living a Good Life; Everything Is F*cked: A Book About Hope*, Mark Manson.

Transitions: Making Sense of Life's Changes, William Bridges.

*Unfu*k Yourself: Get Out of Your Head and into Your Life*, Gary John Bishop.

Untamed, Glennon Doyle

PROFESSIONAL

Below are some of the professional resources that I have found to be helpful. They ultimately confirmed what I was doing was working or challenged me to update my processes. As a stylist, business owner, and human, I don't want to be complacent in my mindset or art.

Beauty-Specific Coaches and Programs

The Thriving Stylist, Britt Seva

thrivingstylist.com

Passion Squared, Nina L. Kovner

passionsquared.net

Nina Tulio

nintulio.com

Geno Stampora

genostampora.com

Slice Squad Consulting

nickiwildflower.com

Beauty of Wealth

beautyofwealth.com

Destroy the Hairdresser

destroythehairdresser.com

It's Mr J Ladner, Joshua Ladner

jladner.com

Independent Stylist podcast, Jennifer Kenny

jenkenny.com

Non-Industry Coaching Resource

Etta Jacobs, MA.

Founder, executive and career transition coaching, Hermes Path.

hermespath.com

Social Media Content Creator Resources

It's Jodie Brown

https://www.aligncreativeco.com/contentservices

Jamie Dana

jamiedana.lpages.co

Social Suite

Ashleighbailey.consulting